TRENT C. BUTLER

A Lesson Commentary for Use with
the International Sunday School Lessons

1999-2000

POINTS

FOR EMPHASIS

BROADMAN
&HOLMAN
PUBLISHERS

Nashville, Tennessee

Dedicated to the devoted friends of Brentwood Baptist Church and the special Sunday school class who have encouraged and supported me through the trials and opportunities of the last few years and who have always rejoiced with me in the publication of a new Points for Emphasis.

Table of Contents

vi   Contents

■ Alternative Lesson for January 16

■ INTRODUCTION

Do you like Bible studies you can apply to your life immediately? Read on. You have a year's worth of materials that want to grab hold of your life and never let you go until you have let God's Word penetrate your soul, purify your heart, and permeate your daily walk.

The first quarter centers on God's premier events for Israel, freeing them from Egypt, transforming slaves into a nation, making His covenant with them, identifying them as a kingdom of priests, a holy nation, and leading them into the promised land. One problem: Israel murmured all the way. Measure your murmuring quotient!

Then turn to the central act of God for all of us: the birth, ministry, death, and resurrection of Jesus of Nazareth, our Lord and Savior. Is He your Savior? Are you sure you are headed to heaven with Him? Is He your Lord? Are you sure you are walking daily with Him?

In the final two quarters of lessons, Paul pounds home the message of God's desire for unity, obedience, and loving service from His people. Get with a Bible study group from your church and see if your church fits Paul's definition of church. Then get with your family and see if your family members think your family meets Paul's definition of family. Don't just read these lessons. Apply them.

God Calls Moses

Basic Passage: Exodus 3:1–2

Who are we? Israel could always answer that question. They simply told a story, the story of their history (see Exod. 12:26, 27; 13:14, 15; Deut. 6:20, 21; Josh. 4:6, 7, 21–23). Fathers told children. Priests told worshipers. Educators told students. That story centered on two events: the exodus from Egypt and the conquest of the Promised Land under Joshua. This quarter we become Israelite children listening to our forefathers tell their story one more time. As we do, we hear the identity of the people of God and decide, Do I want to be that kind of person?

■ THE BIBLE LESSON

Exodus 3

1 Now Moses kept the flock of Jethro his father-in-law, the priest of Midian: and he led the flock to the backside of the desert, and came to the mountain of God, even to Horeb.

2 And the angel of the LORD appeared unto him in a flame of fire out of the midst of a bush: and he looked, and, behold, the bush burned with fire, and the bush was not consumed.

3 And Moses said, I will now turn aside, and see this great sight, why the bush is not burnt.

4 And when the LORD saw that he turned aside to see, God called unto him out of the midst of the bush, and said, Moses, Moses. And he said, Here am I.

5 And he said, Draw not nigh hither: put off thy shoes from off thy feet, for the place whereon thou standest is holy ground.

6 Moreover he said, I am the God of thy father, the God of Abraham, the God of Isaac, and the God of Jacob. And Moses hid his face; for he was afraid to look upon God.

7 And the LORD said, I have surely seen the affliction of my people which are in Egypt, and have heard their cry by reason of their taskmasters; for I know their sorrows;

8 And I am come down to deliver them out of the hand of the Egyptians, and to bring them up out of that land unto a good land and a large, unto a land flowing with milk and honey; unto the place of the Canaanites, and the Hittites, and the Amorites, and the Perizzites, and the Hivites, and the Jebusites.

9 Now therefore, behold, the cry of the children of Israel is come unto me: and I have also seen the oppression wherewith the Egyptians oppress them.

10 Come now therefore, and I will send thee unto Pharaoh, that thou mayest bring forth my people the children of Israel out of Egypt.

11 And Moses said unto God, Who am I, that I should go unto Pharaoh, and that I should bring forth the children of Israel out of Egypt?

12 And he said, Certainly I will be with thee; and this shall be a token unto thee, that I have sent thee: When thou hast brought forth the people out of Egypt, ye shall serve God upon this mountain.

■ THE LESSON EXPLAINED

Angelic Appearance (3:1–3)

Another day at work here in the lonely desert with these constantly bleating sheep. So different from the early days in Egypt. At Pharaoh's court something was always going on. Now here, Jethro has been so kind to take me in, give me his daughter for a wife (see 2:21), and let me work for him. Somehow, I feel I should be doing more. I cannot forget my people in Egypt.

What is that? A bush is burning here in the desert. That doesn't happen too often. It keeps on burning, never burns up and disappears. Strange doings here. Better investigate this.

God's Glory (3:4–6)

Moses was so intent on the bush, he missed the star of the show. God was there in the form of his messenger.

Finally, God had to speak to draw Moses away from the bush and to Him. Come here, but be careful. This is holy ground, ground where God is present. Make sure you bring nothing impure here. Do what your people do when they enter holy territory. Don't mix unholy ground and holy ground. Take your shoes off (see Josh. 5:15). Show your respect. Listen! I want to introduce Myself to you so we can have a special love relationship together (compare 6:2–8).

I am the God you heard about from your real mother (see Exod. 2:8, 9) and from the Israelites. I am the God of the patriarchs, the One who promised them land and descendants and fame and blessing and mission (Gen. 12:2, 3).

Listening in Love (3:7–9)

These promises I will fulfill—now! I am not blind. I see everything going on in history. My people are crying out in sorrow and pain. Well they should be! The Egyptians are cruel. They make My people suffer beyond all human endurance. This must not continue. I will do something about it. Egypt shall no longer control them. I will give them the land I promised.

Yes, I know that seems impossible now. The land is full of all kinds of people. Some, like the Canaanites, Amorites, and Jebusites, have been there as long as anyone can remember. Others, like the Hittites, have come down from the north country. Be sure! I feel the pain of My people. It is coming to an end. I am here to deliver.

Moses' Mandate (3:10–12)

How am I going to deliver them? you ask. Simple! I am sending you to rescue them. You will bring My family out of Egypt.

Wait a minute. Everything sounded good up until now. How did I suddenly get in the picture? You know I cannot go back to Egypt. They have warrants for my arrest. I am a murderer in their eyes (2:12–15). Besides, I have no experience in this sort of diplomacy and battle. You surely do not mean me, Lord.

Yes, Moses, I mean you. No need to worry. I will be with you. My presence overcomes all lack of experience. My presence takes away fear of enemies. I am calling you to mission. Now come! Do not worry. When it is all over, I will bring you and My people right back here to worship. Then you will know I have done all I promised. Until then, believe My promise, and go to Egypt.

■ TRUTHS TO LIVE BY

Obedience is response to God's call. Relationship with God is a relationship of Lord and servant. You know the Lord is faithful. He knows you better than you know yourself. He knows what you can do. He uses that knowledge as He comes to call you to a task. He expects you to hear His call, talk to Him about it, then obey.

Obedience results from experiencing God. Obedience to God is not following a rule book or a set of customs the church sets out. Obedience grows out of a daily experience with God in Bible study and prayer. There you get to know Him, trust Him, and hear His call. Obedience is person relating to person, not person seeking achievement through obeying rules and laws.

Obedience brings divine rewards. God has blessings in store for you. He waits to distribute them until you seek that experience with Him and obediently set out on the mission to which He calls.

■ A VERSE TO REMEMBER

And God said unto Moses, I AM THAT I AM: and he said, Thus shalt thou say unto the children of Israel, I AM hath sent me unto you.—Exodus 3:14

■ DAILY BIBLE READINGS

Crossing the Red Sea

Basic Passage: Exodus 13:17–22; 14:26–31

Police sirens pierced the darkness. Ambulances raced to the scene and quickly to the hospital. The officer called my mother and reported the news. Your son has turned the car over. He is unconscious in the hospital.

Deliver me! mother must have shouted. How much more can I take? Just a couple of months ago my Jerry dies. Now this!

How many times has life brought you to your knees screaming out these words? Let me count the ways. Children making demands I cannot fulfill. Work pressure demanding more time than I have. Loneliness overcoming my best intentions to be brave and strong. Friends proving to be anything but loyal and true. Daily we need deliverance. Where do we find it?

■ THE BIBLE LESSON

Exodus 13

17 And it came to pass, when Pharaoh had let the people go, that God led them not through the way of the land of the Philistines, although that was near; for God said, Lest peradventure the people repent when they see war, and they return to Egypt:

18 But God led the people about, through the way of the wilderness of the Red sea: and the children of Israel went up harnessed out of the land of Egypt.

19 And Moses took the bones of Joseph with him: for he had straitly sworn the children of Israel, saying, God will surely visit you; and ye shall carry up my bones away hence with you.

20 And they took their journey from Succoth, and encamped in Etham, in the edge of the wilderness.

21 And the LORD went before them by day in a pillar of cloud, to lead them the way; and by night in a pillar of fire, to give them light; to go by day and night:

22 He took not away the pillar of the cloud by day, nor the pillar of fire by night, from before the people.

· ·

Exodus 14

26 And the LORD said unto Moses, Stretch out thine hand over the sea, that the waters may come again upon the Egyptians, upon their chariots, and upon their horsemen.

27 And Moses stretched forth his hand over the sea, and the sea returned to his strength when the morning appeared; and the Egyptians fled against it; and the LORD overthrew the Egyptians in the midst of the sea.

28 And the waters returned, and covered the chariots, and the horsemen, and all the host of Pharaoh that came into the sea after them; there remained not so much as one of them.

29 But the children of Israel walked upon dry land in the midst of the sea; and the waters were a wall unto them on their right hand, and on their left.

30 Thus the LORD saved Israel that day out of the hand of the Egyptians; and Israel saw the Egyptians dead upon the sea shore.

31 And Israel saw that great work which the LORD did upon the Egyptians: and the people feared the LORD, and believed the LORD, and his servant Moses.

■ THE LESSON EXPLAINED

Delivered by God's Presence (13:17–22)

Free at last! Free at last! Now what? What do we do with our freedom? Out of Egypt! Where do we go? How do we get there? Frustrating questions bombarded Israel as soon as they realized God had done what He promised. Pharaoh said, "Leave." Fine and good, but you had to go somewhere.

Israel need not fear. God did more than set them free from Pharaoh. He pointed the way of freedom. Surprise again. He did not lead toward the Promised Land along the international highway. He led east toward the wilderness. Why? He knew His people well. International infants, they knew not the ways of warring nations. Having won freedom from Egypt, they might lose faith before a new enemy. They might decide Egypt was not so bad after all (see 16:3; 17:3).

So to the wilderness they marched, with something to help them remember Egypt—the bones of Joseph (see Gen. 50:25). They need not look back, however. God was marching forward, His presence with Israel was clearly visible in a cloud by day and a pillar of fire by night. Not one second did He disappear. Israel had only to look up. God continued to deliver them.

Delivered by God's Power (14:26–29)

Too good to be true? Egypt will not let us go that easily. Here they come. And here is God, ready to act. Now we will see who has more power: God or Pharaoh. Not much battle strategy here. Moses, stretch your hand out over the sea. Watch the waters. They stood back for us to cross. Now they roar forward again to bury the Egyptians. Oh, the power of our God! He controls the fearful sea. More important, He controls the fearful enemy! Did anyone ever have such a God?

Delivered to Worship God (14:30–31)

No doubt who won this battle. The evidence is clear. We stand on dry ground following God's symbols of presence to the wilderness. The Egyptians lie dead on the seashore. What a glorious God. Come, let us adore Him. Let us worship Him. No one is like Him. We can believe what He says. We can trust Moses as the leader He gave us. Oh, worship the Lord, the God of Israel! He alone delivers His people from all their troubles.

■ TRUTHS TO LIVE BY

God's deliverance does not come in ways we expect. Israel looked to cross the sea and hurry along to the Promised Land. God knew they needed protection from hardships along the international highway. They needed time at the holy mountain to learn His way. About face! To the wilderness. Do not try to predict God. Just follow!

God's deliverance builds on past divine acts. God promised the patriarchs. He brought Joseph to power. He delivered Israel from famine. He led them to Egypt. Now he had them in place for the next mighty act. With God, one deliverance always leads to another. Are you ready?

God's deliverance reveals His powerful presence. Deliverance is not a game that God plays to show off His power every once in a while. Deliverance is the very nature of the God who loves you and wants a love relationship with you. The act of deliverance is not the most important thing with God. Letting you see and respond to His presence is His top priority.

God's deliverance seeks to create faith. Discovering God's presence brings you to your knees in faith and worship. You acknowledge your lack of power to deliver. You praise Him for past deliverance and trust Him to do the same in the future. Deliverance reveals presence, evokes faith, and creates an ongoing relationship of trust.

■ A VERSE TO REMEMBER

And Moses said unto the people, Fear ye not, stand still, and see the salvation of the LORD, which he will shew to you to day: for the Egyptians whom ye have seen today, ye shall see them again no more for ever.—Exodus 14:13

■ DAILY BIBLE READINGS

Sept. 6 — The Festival of Unleavened Bread. Exod. 13:3–10

Sept. 7 — Consecration of the Firstborn. Exod. 13:11–16

Sept. 8 — Led by Pillars of Cloud and Fire. Exod. 13:17–22

Sept. 9 — Caught between Pharaoh and the Sea. Exod. 14:1–9

Sept. 10 — Going Forward at God's Command. Exod. 14:10–18

Sept. 11 — Israel Crosses the Red Sea. Exod. 14:19–25

Sept. 12 — God Saves Israel from the Egyptians. Exod. 14:26–31

The Covenant

Basic Passage: Exodus 19:3–6; 20:2–4, 7, 8, 12–17

Years ago I bought a house in an old established subdivision. When I signed the papers, I found one unexpected one in the bunch—a landowner's covenant. The property owners in the subdivision had an organization that sought to protect the value of property and the beauty of the subdivision. Anyone buying into the subdivision had to sign a covenant promising to keep up the property according to the rules of the subdivision and promising not to build unsightly buildings on the property. I faced the choice freely. Sign the covenant, or do not buy in the subdivision. Having signed the covenant, I then had to obey its stipulations. Otherwise, I faced stiff penalties, up to expulsion from the subdivision.

In a small way this illustrates the decision the children of Israel faced. The house I bought satisfied the needs and tastes of our family. Israel found that God did everything they expected and more. He delivered them from slavery and brought them to safety. He formed a multitude of slaves into a nation. Now He faced them on the mountain with a choice—be My covenant people or choose another god.

■ **THE BIBLE LESSON**

Exodus 19

3 And Moses went up unto God, and the LORD called unto him out of the mountain, saying, Thus shalt thou say to the house of Jacob, and tell the children of Israel;

4 Ye have seen what I did unto the Egyptians, and how I bore you on eagles' wings, and brought you unto myself.

5 Now therefore, if ye will obey my voice indeed, and keep my covenant, then ye shall be a peculiar treasure unto me above all people: for all the earth is mine:

6 And ye shall be unto me a kingdom of priests, and an holy nation. These are the words which thou shalt speak unto the children of Israel.

. . . .

Exodus 20

2 I am the LORD thy God, which have brought thee out of the land of Egypt, out of the house of bondage.

3 Thou shalt have no other gods before me.

4 Thou shalt not make unto thee any graven image, or any likeness of any thing that is in heaven above, or that is in the earth beneath, or that is in the water under the earth:

7 Thou shalt not take the name of the LORD thy God in vain; for the LORD will not hold him guiltless that taketh his name in vain.

8 Remember the sabbath day, to keep it holy.

12 Honour thy father and thy mother: that thy days may be long upon the land which the LORD thy God giveth thee.

13 Thou shalt not kill.

14 Thou shalt not commit adultery.

15 Thou shalt not steal.

16 Thou shalt not bear false witness against thy neighbour.

17 Thou shalt not covet thy neighbour's house, thou shalt not covet thy neighbour's wife, nor his manservant, nor his maidservant, nor his ox, nor his ass, nor any thing that is thy neighbour's.

▊ THE LESSON EXPLAINED

God's Peculiar Treasure (19:3–6)

A nation rejoicing over unexpected victory at the sea. A nation wondering where they were going. A nation, most of all, seeking identity. No longer slaves bound to a foreign power, they needed a sense of who they were or at least who they were becoming. They had no way of knowing. God did. He knew their perplexity. He knew the solution. Since He is a loving God, He took the initiative to answer the people's questions.

He called Moses His servant with a message for His people. You are a saved people. I brought you out of Egypt. You are a presence people, for I have brought you here to My mountain to be with Me. You are My people. You owe everything you are and have to what I have done for you. Should be no question then. You are an obedient people. You trust Me and depend on Me for guidance and direction. An obedient people becomes something else: a special, treasured people. Literally, you are My own possession.

I have a relationship with you unlike My relationship with any other people on earth. I created the earth. It belongs to Me. All its people belong to me, but none in the way you belong to Me. For I have a special calling for you. You really expect to go into the land I am going to show you and become a dominant political power like the Egyptians? That is not what I want. You are to be priests for me. Yes, everyone in the nation is to be My priest. Just as priests give up land rights and other personal privileges to take care of My sanctuary and to offer sacrifices for your sins and to teach you My word, so you will give up political power and its privileges.

You will introduce all the nations to Me. You will let them know who I am. You will do what is necessary to bring forgiveness and atonement for them, just as your priests do for you. To do this, you have to live a different kind of life, a life separated out to God, a life pure of sin, a life showing the world what I am like. Now here is what it means to be a holy, separated, pure nation.

God's Peculiar Position (20:2–4)

My peculiar treasure understands one thing: I am your God. I am different from all other gods. I proved My power and My care for you in the Exodus from Egypt. You do not need any other God. I can satisfy all the needs you think another god might satisfy. You need no picture of Me. I am Creator, not created. Nothing in the created world can adequately portray who I am. Anything you make will tempt you to think you can control what you've made. None of that. That is the way pagan nations worship. I am the invisible God who is always present with you. That is My position. It is unchangeable. Worship Me under My conditions, for I proved Myself in the Exodus. Trust me.

God's Peculiar Name (20:7, 8)

Moses told you how I revealed My special name to him (Exod. 3:13–15). I let you know My personal, special name, in Hebrew *Yahweh,* meaning I AM WHO I AM. That name shows I have sovereign control. No one else can influence who I am or what I do. Yet I have let you know My holy name. I trust you with it. You must not use it loosely. I give you the name so you can know Me fully, worship Me reverently, and call on Me trustingly. I do not give it to you to use selfishly. No curses on the enemy. No magic formulas. No attempt to manipulate the name for your own advantage. You are My priests worshiping Me and blessing other nations (Gen. 12:1–3). You are not the winners of a lucky drawing, getting a prize you can use to depend on your own resources. You are wholly dependent on Me. You have My name to bless Me, not to control Me.

You bless Me through worship. One day a week is set aside for rest from normal activities and dedication to my activities. On that day, especially, you will use My name in worship, but use it carefully. On the Sabbath find rest for your bodies and for your souls, as you rest yourself in Me.

God's Peculiar Expectations (20:12–17)

Special instructions for dealing with Me. Also special instructions for dealing with other people. Yes, My covenant involves more than being true in your relationship with Me. It also means treating other people right. This starts with your family. Parents brought you into the world, fed you, taught you, loved you, introduced you to Me. Now put them in the place of importance in your life that they deserve. And I do not mean just when you are children. All your life, you owe who you are to your parents. Take care of them, give them love, make them feel important, for they are the most important people in your lives. Then you will be My covenant people experiencing My covenant blessings.

Do nothing to harm someone else or take away their dignity. Of course, you will not kill anyone. You will protect your own family by remaining true to the one you married. No fooling around outside marriage! No, never at all for any reason. Be content with what you have. Do not try to take away what someone else has either by deed or word. Do not steal property. Do not steal reputation with false witness in court. Show love to other people by protecting their reputation in the community. It all begins with your thinking processes. You see something your neighbor has. You like it. Then you begin admiring it and talking about it. Then you wish you had one like it. Then you decide you could use it better than the neighbor does. So, finally you take it. Do not let the process get started. Tell your neighbor good things about what they have, and leave it at that. Do not covet.

Yes, be My people. Relate to Me and to other people as I tell you. I deserve it. They deserve it. You will find life richer, fuller, and happier. You will be My people, My peculiar possession. What other identity could you want?

■ TRUTHS TO LIVE BY

Covenant call is a call to special responsibility. To be God's people is the greatest privilege on earth. Nothing is better for you than to be in that close personal relationship with Him. To be that close to Him means to act like Him, to be holy as He is holy. If you want to be near Him and know His blessings, you must act like Him. The two are different sides of the same person.

Covenant call is a call to special relationship. God wants you to know Him as intimately as possible. He wants you to experience His loving presence every day, all day. He is always available. Are you?

Covenant call is a call to special regulations. God knows what is best for your life in relationship to Him and to other people. Thus, He sets out regulations for you to live by. Follow them and experience Him.

■ A VERSE TO REMEMBER

Now therefore, if ye will obey my voice indeed, and keep my covenant, then ye shall be a peculiar treasure unto me above all people: for all the earth is mine.—Exodus 19:5

■ DAILY BIBLE READINGS

Sept. 13— Israel Camps at Mount Sinai. Exod. 19:1–9
Sept. 14— Moses Consecrates the People. Exod. 19:10–15
Sept. 15— Israel meets God at Mount Sinai.
            Exod. 19:16–25
Sept. 16— Honor God and Keep the Sabbath.
            Exod. 20:1–11
Sept. 17— Commandments for Life in Community.
            Exod. 20:12–21
Sept. 18— Observe God's Statutes and Ordinances.
            Deut. 4:1–8
Sept. 19— Teach Obedience to Generations That Follow.
            Deut. 4:9–14

The Tabernacle and Obedience

Basic Passage: Exodus 40:1–9; Leviticus 26:2–6, 11–13

Unforgettable memories! We all have them. Among mine will always be the first church I saw in Kenya. Our little unit of three missions volunteers followed our newly met Kenyan friends up the little path, under the tree branches, through the fork in the road. Could not tell we were getting anywhere. Suddenly, a new fork in the road, and before us stood a lovely thatched building.

Our hosts joyously opened the door and invited us in to the seats of honor. A few chairs and benches were carefully in order in front of the pulpit. Curious Kenyans came to see the first white people many of them had ever seen. Then they started singing. Then they told with great pride how an elder of the church had donated the land, and the people had built the church. They, unlike many of their neighbors, had their own place to worship. Hallelujah! Later, we found out that for less than $1,000 we could make sure the neighbors had resources to build their churches. As you read this, I will have returned to Kenya and seen new churches we helped our Kenyan friends build. They help me understand the feelings Israel had as they dedicated their newly built place of worship.

■ THE BIBLE LESSON

Exodus 40

1 And the LORD spake unto Moses, saying,

2 On the first day of the first month shalt thou set up the tabernacle of the tent of the congregation.

3 And thou shalt put therein the ark of the testimony, and cover the ark with the veil.

4 And thou shalt bring in the table, and set in order the things that are to be set in order upon it; and thou shalt bring in the candlestick, and light the lamps thereof.

5 And thou shalt set the altar of gold for the incense before the ark of the testimony, and put the hanging of the door to the tabernacle.

6 And thou shalt set the altar of the burnt offering before the door of the tabernacle of the tent of the congregation.

7 And thou shalt set the laver between the tent of the congregation and the altar, and shalt put water therein.

8 And thou shalt set up the court round about, and hang up the hanging at the court gate.

9 And thou shalt take the anointing oil, and anoint the tabernacle, and all that is therein, and shalt hallow it, and all the vessels thereof: and it shall be holy.

. . . .

Leviticus 26

2 Ye shall keep my sabbaths, and reverence my sanctuary: I am the LORD.

3 If ye walk in my statutes, and keep my commandments, and do them;

4 Then I will give you rain in due season, and the land shall yield her increase, and the trees of the field shall yield their fruit.

5 And your threshing shall reach unto the vintage, and the vintage shall reach unto the sowing time: and ye shall eat your bread to the full, and dwell in your land safely.

6 And I will give peace in the land, and ye shall lie down, and none shall make you afraid: and I will rid evil beasts out of the land, neither shall the sword go through your land.

11 And I will set my tabernacle among you: and my soul shall not abhor you.

12 And I will walk among you, and will be your God, and ye shall be my people.

13 I am the LORD your God, which brought you forth out of the land of Egypt, that ye should not be their bondmen; and I have broken the bands of your yoke, and made you go upright.

■ **THE LESSON EXPLAINED**

Establishing the Holy Place (Exod. 40:1–9)

The long, hard work is complete. The huge tent of worship is ready for use. God gives the command: Set up the tent! The innermost part will contain the ark of the testimony, which you also call the ark of the covenant. My tablets with the Ten Commandments are in the ark. They remind you as you look to the tent that God has a covenant relationship with you which promises His presence and expects your grateful obedience. The veil separates the innermost holy of holies from the rest of the holy space. Only once a year will someone push back the veil and enter in. That reminds you how precious and costly atonement is and how holy and pure God is.

I have given you instructions about all the equipment. Place it just where I say. Each piece represents something about My presence with you, My saving deeds for you, and My worship expectations of you. Then Moses, you are to take the holy anointing oil and symbolically dedicate the tabernacle and its worship to Me. Then all the people will know this is My special meeting place with My people. They shall see that I have made it holy, separated out for My service. Having set up the tent, you can worship Me just as I want you to.

Revering the Holy Place (Lev. 26:2–6)

Having a dedicated place of worship does not guarantee anything. With the structure, you must also have the attitude. You must show how important worship is by separating one day out of the week to worship rather than work. Six days you have to make a living. One day I have for your complete attention and devotion. Then you shall let the priests carry out the Sabbath day duties of worship. You shall have holy fear, awe, and respect for this worship place I have set up for you. You shall do nothing to bring dishonor or disrespect or impurity on it. It is My holy place of worship. Treat it as such. This is the only place you have to worship. I will give you the rain and the products of your farm labors and your food and your safety and security. Armies will not hurt you; neither will wild animals. I am your protector. Have no fear. Fear no other gods. I am the Creator, able to give all you need.

Revealing God in the Holy Place (Lev. 26:11–13)

Why have a place of worship? It shows God's presence and God's care. When God lets His dwelling place stand right where you live, He shows He is willing to live where you live. Such a God loves you and cannot hate you. You can know Him, who He is, and what He stands for, because He walks in your midst. He gives the covenant promise to you: He will be your God, and you will be His people. Always remember, you surely want Him and no one else to be your God. He is the One and the only One who brought you out of slavery in Egypt and created you as His special possession, His peculiar treasure, His people. There's the tent. That means, here's God. Where are you? Walking with Him? Or . . . ?

■ TRUTHS TO LIVE BY

God's holy worship place reflects God's nature. It does matter what a worship place looks like. No, not how expensive and modern and extravagant it looks. It matters how neat, cared-for, and clean it looks. God is perfect purity and holiness. His worship place should let every one who sees it know this much about God.

God's holy worship place deserves human respect and reverence. The worship place is the place for activities with God. It is set apart for one purpose: worship. Other places may be used for fun and games, building fellowship and community. The worship place holds only memories of worship, of being in touch with God, of walking with God, of learning about God as He reveals Himself to you. Every action in the worship place is an act of worship.

God's holy place represents God's presence with His people. The place of worship is not a monument to human wealth, artistry, and accomplishment. It is an opportunity for holy moments, moments when you know you are meeting God and letting His presence change your life. If you do not meet God there, you have no need for a worship place, and the worship place is not serving the purpose God intends for it to serve.

■ A VERSE TO REMEMBER

Ye shall keep my sabbaths, and reverence my sanctuary: I am the LORD.—*Leviticus 26:2*

■ DAILY BIBLE READINGS

Sept. 20— God's Command Regarding Tabernacle and Priests. Exod. 40:1–15
Sept. 21— Building the Tabernacle. Exod. 40:16–23
Sept. 22— Equipping the Tabernacle. Exod. 40:24–33
Sept. 23— Rewards for Obedience. Lev. 26:1–13
Sept. 24— Consequences for Disobedience. Lev. 26:14–22
Sept. 25— Disobedience Will Bring Horrible Punishment. Lev. 26:23–33
Sept. 26— Confession Will Bring Renewal. Lev. 26:34–46

The Cloud and the Fire

Basic Passage: Exodus 40:34–38; Numbers 9:15–19, 22–23

Mission trips teach me how to follow God day by day. As a sophomore in college, I trekked out to Colorado to do summer missions. Suddenly alone for the first time in my life and expected to go door to door canvassing people for a church I had never attended, I turned quickly to God. Each evening I said, *This is the last time, God.* Each morning I said, *Give me strength and your presence for one more day, God.* I saw no mystical cloud in the sky. No fireball appeared by night. Still, I never doubted. God was there.

Then only last summer in Kenya, I repeated the same experience. Found anew and afresh how dear God's presence is. The territory may be gorgeous Colorado or exotically beautiful Kenya. The people may speak your language and follow your customs or may enjoy a totally different lifestyle. Still when you are living in strange territory among strangers, you gratefully learn that no land is strange to God and no people or language can shut out His presence.

■ THE BIBLE LESSON

Exodus 40

34 Then a cloud covered the tent of the congregation, and the glory of the LORD filled the tabernacle.

35 And Moses was not able to enter into the tent of the congregation, because the cloud abode thereon, and the glory of the LORD filled the tabernacle.

36 And when the cloud was taken up from over the tabernacle, the children of Israel went onward in all their journeys:

37 But if the cloud were not taken up, then they journeyed not till the day that it was taken up.

38 For the cloud of the LORD was upon the tabernacle by day, and fire was on it by night, in the sight of all the house of Israel, throughout all their journeys.

. . . .

Numbers 9

15 And on the day that the tabernacle was reared up the cloud covered the tabernacle, namely, the tent of the testimony: and at even there was upon the tabernacle as it were the appearance of fire, until the morning.

16 So it was alway: the cloud covered it by day, and the appearance of fire by night.

17 And when the cloud was taken up from the tabernacle, then after that the children of Israel journeyed: and in the place where the cloud abode, there the children of Israel pitched their tents.

18 At the commandment of the LORD the children of Israel journeyed, and at the commandment of the LORD they pitched: as long as the cloud abode upon the tabernacle they rested in their tents.

19 And when the cloud tarried long upon the tabernacle many days, then the children of Israel kept the charge of the LORD, and journeyed not.

22 Or whether it were two days, or a month, or a year, that the cloud tarried upon the tabernacle, remaining thereon, the children of Israel abode in their tents, and journeyed not: but when it was taken up, they journeyed.

23 At the commandment of the LORD they rested in the tents, and at the commandment of the LORD they journeyed: they kept the charge of the LORD, at the commandment of the LORD by the hand of Moses.

■ THE LESSON EXPLAINED

Follow the Glory (40:34–38)

We have done our part. Gave all the treasures we had. Worked as hard as we knew how. The tabernacle is finished. Now what will happen to us out here in this mountain wilderness of strange weather, strange people—what few there are—and strange animals? Are we safe here? Or would life in Egypt with all its trials have been safer and more secure?

Look! Did you see that? A cloud out of heaven came down and sat on top of God's tabernacle. A strange bright glow emanates from the tent. Moses wants to go in and see what is happening, but something stops him. He can go no further. God is in His tabernacle. That is God's glory.

What a marvelous reality, God's glory. You know, literally it means, His weight, His heaviness. When we see His glory, we know He is throwing His weight, His importance, His reputation around for us. He is on our side. What else could we want?

Just like He led us in the Exodus, He is still leading us (see Exod. 13:21, 22; 14:19, 24;16:10; 24:16–18; 33:9–10, 22; 34:5). We are safe with God.

Look, the cloud is moving. That means it's time for us to move too. Let's get packing. We have no reason to fear. God has proved Himself faithful again. We should need no more proof. Just follow Him day by day.

Follow by Moving Forward (Numbers 9:15–17)

Life can be fairly simple. God knows what is best. God knows where is best. God knows when is best. God does not keep this a big secret, laughing up His sleeve because you do not know. No! God wants you to know what is best for you to do, what is best for you to have, when is best for you to act, and where the best place is for you to be. He made the choice rather easy for Israel. He made His presence clear. He made His leadership decisions clear. Look to the sky over the tabernacle. God sat there in the cloud or in the nightly fireball. Occasionally, God chose to move to the next camping ground. Then the cloud or the pillar of fire took off. Israel had to follow close behind. Suddenly, the cloud would stop. Israel did too. The cloud no longer stands before us, but God's Spirit abides in us, giving the same leadership today, if we will listen to His still, small voice.

Follow by Standing Still (9:18, 19, 22, 23)

Following God is not always action-centered. Often, God wants us to stand still and wait. Israel, chomping at the bit to find a new homeland and settle in for the long haul, learned patience. God was not always ready to lead them home. He had lessons for them to learn in the lonely deserted wilderness. So often, the cloud tarried over the tabernacle—a day, a month, a year. When it did, Israel stayed put, waiting to hear God's instructions and learning to develop patience with God. His timetable differed radically from theirs. His had to rule. Priority was not occupying territory and finding a new home. Priority was learning obedience.

■ TRUTHS TO LIVE BY

We follow God only when we experience His presence. Often, we want to set up a list of rules and regulations that show us we are obedient and faithful. God does not play the rules game. He plays only the presence game. He wants you to recognize His presence with you, experience Him in the fullness of His indwelling Spirit, and follow as the Spirit gives you the experience of knowing God's when, what, and where, even if you do not know His why.

We follow God by moving at His command. God has raised Henry Blackaby and his *Experiencing God* teachings to help our generation learn this lesson anew. We do not get a committee, decide what needs to be done, start the program rolling, and then ask God to bless it with His presence. We learn to obey God and experience His fullness. Then He shows us where He is and how He is acting. We join in.

We follow God by waiting for Him to speak. An action generation learns the waiting lesson slowly and impatiently. God's goal for Israel was always to give them rest. We, too, often, want Him to give us work. God speaks to a people at rest, preparing them for His time of action. Listen to His voice while you can. Stand at attention to move only when He gives the command, "Forward, march!"

■ A VERSE TO REMEMBER

For the cloud of the LORD was upon the tabernacle by day, and fire was on it by night, in the sight of all the house of Israel, throughout all their journeys.—Exodus 40:38

■ DAILY BIBLE READINGS

Sept. 27— God's Glory Fills the Tabernacle.
Exod. 40:34–38
Sept. 28— Led by God's Cloud and Fire. Num. 9:15–23
Sept. 29— Journeying Away from Mount Sinai.
Num. 10:11, 12, 33–36
Sept. 30— God Keeps Covenant Forever. Ps. 105:1–15
Oct. 1   — God Provided for Israel in Egypt.
Ps. 105:16–25
Oct. 2   — God Sent Plagues upon Egypt.
Ps. 105:26–36
Oct. 3   — God Delivered Israel from Egypt.
Ps. 105:37–45

The People Rebel

Basic Passage: Numbers 13:1–3, 32–14:4, 20–24

Teenage rebellion! We talk about it all the time. Parents with teenagers, especially. Experts now say extended life expectancy has expanded the teenage years through age 29 or so. That's not new to God. So many of us have expanded our teenage rebellion years with Him, far beyond age 29. How I rebelled when it became obvious He was calling me back to Nashville, to work at the institution where my father-in-law had become a legend in thirty-five dedicated years of labor. Anywhere but there, I had promised through the years. With His marvelous sense of humor, God sent me THERE. Now, after eighteen years, I clearly see why God wanted me here. But He got me here only after months of rebellion on my part!

■ THE BIBLE LESSON

Numbers 13

1 And the LORD spake unto Moses, saying,

2 Send thou men, that they may search the land of Canaan, which I give unto the children of Israel: of every tribe of their fathers shall ye send a man, every one a ruler among them.

3 And Moses by the commandment of the LORD sent them from the wilderness of Paran: all those men were heads of the children of Israel.

32 And they brought up an evil report of the land which they had searched unto the children of Israel, saying, The land, through which we have gone to search it, is a land that eateth up the inhabitants thereof; and all the people that we saw in it are men of a great stature.

33 And there we saw the giants, the sons of Anak, which come of the giants: and we were in our own sight as grasshoppers, and so we were in their sight.

. . . .

Numbers 14

1 And all the congregation lifted up their voice, and cried; and the people wept that night.

2 And all the children of Israel murmured against Moses and against Aaron: and the whole congregation said unto them, Would God that we had died in the land of Egypt! or would God we had died in this wilderness!

3 And wherefore hath the LORD brought us unto this land, to fall by the sword, that our wives and our children should be a prey? Were it not better for us to return into Egypt?

4 And they said one to another, Let us make a captain, and let us return into Egypt.

20 And the LORD said, I have pardoned according to thy word:

21 But as truly as I live, all the earth shall be filled with the glory of the LORD.

22 Because all those men which have seen my glory, and my miracles, which I did in Egypt and in the wilderness, and have tempted me now these ten times, and have not hearkened to my voice:

23 Surely they shall not see the land which I sware unto their fathers, neither shall any of them that provoked me see it:

24 But my servant Caleb, because he had another spirit with him, and hath followed me fully, him will I bring into the land whereinto he went; and his seed shall possess it.

■ THE LESSON EXPLAINED

The Search Party's Selection (13:1–3)

What an assignment! Here we are in the wilderness of Paran, north of Sinai, west of Edom, south and west of the Dead Sea, and just south of the Promised Land (see Gen. 14:6; 21:21; Exod. 15:15; Num. 12:16; Deut. 1:22; 1 Kings 11:17). After all these months in the wilderness, finally we get to see the land God has promised. Lucky twelve will get a foretaste. God has chosen them as spies to see the land and tell us all about its luxurious provisions ready for us to occupy. Can't wait to hear their report.

The Search Party's Suspicion (13:32–14:4)

Moses, we did not expect this! We did our job thoroughly, spent forty days in the Promised Land (see v. 25). Beautiful land! Never saw such grapes and fruits and crops! Oh, to be able to farm such fertile ground! We can never make it, Moses! People live there already. Not just any people, but a huge, strong, well-armed, well-defended people. No one could ever take the land away from them. They are too strong for us. Sure, Caleb can spout his beautiful pious phrases about all we can do, but we must be realistic. Giants live in the land. Leave it alone! They are called the sons of Anak, or Anakim. Their ancestors are the famous giants (Heb. *Nephilim*). You know their story. They go clear back to Noah's days (Gen. 6:4; compare Deut. 1:28; 2:10, 11, 21; 9:2; Josh. 11:21, 22; 14:12, 15; 15:13, 14; 21:11; Judg. 1:20).

Moses, the spies are right. Why did you ever tempt us to leave Egypt? Oh, that we had died there, or even in the wilderness of Sinai, before we got here where those giants can get us. What is this Yahweh up to anyway? Will He enjoy seeing our wives and kids abused and slaughtered? Who will lead us? Reverse march! Back to Egypt!

The Search Party's Sentence (14:20–24)

God, what now? Yes, your servant Moses sees your glory among us, but it is different. You are intent on killing Your rebellious people. We deserve it, but don't do it. Protect Your name among all the nations of Canaan. They have already heard about You. Forgive us. Do no harm to us. Please, Lord.

You are forgiven, just as you asked. But forgiveness is not My only word here. The guilty must be punished. I will swear to that on My own life. It is as sure as the fact that one day My glory, yes, the shining, visible presence of God Himself, will fill not just the tabernacle but the whole earth (compare Exod. 40:34, 35; 1 Kings 8:11; Ezek. 10:4; 43:5; 44:4; Ps. 72:19; Hab. 2:14; Isa. 6:3). You know I will fulfill my purpose. I will also fulfill this punishment. These spies saw My glorious presence entering the tabernacle. They saw the miracles I did in the Exodus and in the wilderness, bringing victory over enemies and provisions for daily life. Still, over and over they tempt and test and try Me. Enough! No spy will see the Promised Land. No one who believed their report and protested against Me, wanting to return to Egypt, will see the land. But Caleb will. He obeyed Me. He is a different kind of person. I shall take him into the land and give him and his descendants an inheritance in it. I reward obedience and faithfulness. I punish rebellion.

■ TRUTHS TO LIVE BY

God chooses people for specific tasks. God wanted Israel to see the land and get excited about occupying it. So He called out men to spy it out for His people. He continues to work in His church, showing the church where He is at work and calling out individuals to join Him in the work He is doing.

Rebel eyes do not see God's opportunities. God-chosen people can rebel against the One who chose them. They may not have faith to see what God plans to do and what He can do. They may look with realistic human eyes rather than trusting eyes of faith.

Rebel actions bring divine punishment. Forgiveness does not mean immediate forgetfulness. God punishes sinners. They have to endure the result of unfaithful choices. Spies lost the opportunity to live in the fruitful land God had prepared for them. You may face punishment for not joining God in the task He has shown you He is involved in.

■ A VERSE TO REMEMBER

If the LORD delight in us, then he will bring us into this land, and give it us; a land which floweth with milk and honey. Only rebel not ye against the LORD, neither fear ye the people of the land; for they are bread for us: their defence is departed from them, and the LORD is with us: fear them not.—Numbers 14:8, 9

DAILY BIBLE READINGS

Oct. 4 — Aaron and Miriam Jealous of Moses.
Num. 12:1–9

Oct. 5 — Miriam Punished with Leprosy.
Num. 12:10–15

Oct. 6 — Twelve Sent to Spy out Canaan.
Num. 13:1–16

Oct. 7 — The Spies Carry out Moses' Orders.
Num. 13:17–24

Oct. 8 — Fearful Spies and a Negative Report.
Num. 13:25–33

Oct. 9 — Israel Rebels against Moses and Aaron.
Num. 14:1–12

Oct. 10 — Moses Intercedes for Israel. Num. 14:13–25

The Desert Years

Basic Passage: Deuteronomy 1:41–44; 2:1–7, 16–18

Where is God when I need Him? How many times have we asked this presumptuous, theologically-illiterate, but emotionally ever-present question? My wife's death certainly brought this question to my lips numerous times. So have many other much less radical experiences. Even now as I write these materials, I search for God's direction in church service. For the first time in over fifteen years, I have no class to teach, no support group to enjoy, no specific place of ministry. God is trying to say something. I am not hearing well. Spiritual dryness in ministry does not suit me well. Am I uncomfortable with God's rest? Am I impatient for God's will? Am I simply too hard on myself? Lord, help me to endure the desert years so I will be ready for your time of victory and rest!

■ THE BIBLE LESSON

Deuteronomy 1

41 Then ye answered and said unto me, We have sinned against the LORD, we will go up and fight, according to all that the LORD our God commanded us. And when ye had girded on every man his weapons of war, ye were ready to go up into the hill.

42 And the LORD said unto me, Say unto them, Go not up, neither fight; for I am not among you; lest ye be smitten before your enemies.

43 So I spake unto you; and ye would not hear, but rebelled against the commandment of the LORD, and went presumptuously up into the hill.

44 And the Amorites, which dwelt in that mountain, came out against you, and chased you, as bees do, and destroyed you in Seir, even unto Hormah.

Deuteronomy 2

1 Then we turned, and took our journey into the wilderness by the way of the Red sea, as the LORD spake unto me: and we compassed mount Seir many days.

2 And the LORD spake unto me, saying,

3 Ye have compassed this mountain long enough: turn you northward.

4 And command thou the people, saying, Ye are to pass through the coast of your brethren the children of Esau, which dwell in Seir; and they shall be afraid of you: take ye good heed unto yourselves therefore;

5 Meddle not with them; for I will not give you of their land, no, not so much as a foot breadth; because I have given mount Seir unto Esau for a possession.

6 Ye shall buy meat of them for money, that ye may eat; and ye shall also buy water of them for money, that ye may drink.

7 For the LORD thy God hath blessed thee in all the works of thy hand: he knoweth thy walking through this great wilderness: these forty years the LORD thy God hath been with thee; thou hast lacked nothing.

16 So it came to pass, when all the men of war were consumed and dead from among the people,

17 That the Lord spake unto me, saying,

18 Thou art to pass over through Ar, the coast of Moab, this day.

■ THE LESSON EXPLAINED

Wilderness Defeat (1:41–44)

Memories. What do they teach us? In the Book of Deuteronomy, God, through Moses, called Israel to remember the good times as well as the bad. Had a new generation primed to enter the Promised Land learned the lesson of obedience the dead generation had not learned? God intended these wilderness years to be romance years, the wooing of God and people into an eternal relationship of love and faithful obedience. Instead, they turned into murmuring years, rebelling against God's way of guiding history.

Punished for listening to the spies' unbelieving and fearful report, the people compounded the sin by declaring war and marching forward to battle, strictly disobeying God's orders (see Num. 14:41–45). The predictable result: disastrous defeat.

Wilderness Blessing (2:1–7)

A punished people finally listened to God's voice, watched for God's leading presence, and went where He wanted them to be (compare 1:40 and 2:1). God's way was not Israel's. They wanted to go due north to Hormah, near Arad and Beersheba (1:44). God led them the long way around, going north but also east, to the other side of the Jordan River by a circuitous route that bypassed enemy Edom (see vv. 5, 6). Now the people could travel God's road in God's way, without fear.

Traveling life God's way brings a new attitude. Memories forget bad times and rebellious times and see that in the overall picture, life in the desert has been a life of blessing, receiving everything needed from the hand of God. Forty years of history depended totally on the divine supply system. It never failed.

Wilderness Expectation (2:16–18)

Finally, "Forward March!" God's command resounded through the wilderness. Israel knew the moment was almost at hand. The Promised Land would become the possessed land. So they moved toward Moab. Finally, God had a people ready to go where He led and to do what He commanded when He told them to.

■ TRUTHS TO LIVE BY

Doing God's purpose at the wrong time is sin. God's promise will be fulfilled, but on His conditions. You cannot refuse to do His will today and then try to make up for it tomorrow. You must be aware of what God is up to now and join Him in it. If now is punishment time, you must endure punishment until God gives the orders to act according to His plan.

Life's worst circumstances are God's opportunities for blessing. God works in the wilderness as well as in the oasis. Circumstances do not determine whether He can or will bless us. We need to be alert to His blessings and respond in gratitude and obedience.

Life's waiting times prepare you for God's victory times. The desert appears to offer little joy or hope. The desert offers time to be with God and experience the fullness of His glory. That experience prepares you to respond to victory as God wants you to respond, walking in the same faith and obedience you learned in the desert.

■ A VERSE TO REMEMBER

For the LORD thy God hath blessed thee in all the works of thy hand: he knoweth thy walking through this great wilderness: these forty years the LORD thy God hath been with thee; thou hast lacked nothing.—Deuteronomy 2:7

■ DAILY BIBLE READINGS

Oct. 11 — Moses Reminds Israel about Horeb.
　　　　　Deut. 1:1-8
Oct. 12 — Tribal Leaders Were Appointed.
　　　　　Deut. 1:9-18
Oct. 13 — Israel Refused to Obey God.
　　　　　Deut. 1:19-33
Oct. 14 — Israel Was Punished for Disobedience.
　　　　　Deut. 1:34-45
Oct. 15 — Israel Wandered in the Wilderness.
　　　　　Deut. 1:46-2:13a
Oct. 16 — A Generation of Warriors Passed Away.
　　　　　Deut. 2:13b-25
Oct. 17 — Israel Began the Conquest of Canaan.
　　　　　Deut. 2:26-37

The Great Commandment

Basic Passage: Deuteronomy 6:1–9, 20–24

Dad had one lesson I will never forget. As I worked with and for him in the grocery store accounting office, I had to take money from people as they paid their monthly (or yearly) bill. That meant I had to put the money they gave me in the cash drawer and give them proper change. Dad's words rang clear: At the end of the day, the cash drawer must balance to the penny. How many days I fussed and fumed trying to get Dad to be satisfied with a cash drawer that was one nickel over. Too often, my relationship with God is similar. I fuss and fume trying to find some way to get around His expectations. Meanwhile, He repeats the same commandment over and over—what Jesus called the greatest of commandments: Love Me.

■ THE BIBLE LESSON

Deuteronomy 6

1 Now these are the commandments, the statutes, and the judgments, which the LORD your God commanded to teach you, that ye might do them in the land whither ye go to possess it:

2 That thou mightest fear the LORD thy God, to keep all his statutes and his commandments, which I command thee, thou, and thy son, and thy son's son, all the days of thy life; and that thy days may be prolonged.

3 Hear therefore, O Israel, and observe to do it; that it may be well with thee, and that ye may increase mightily, as the LORD God of thy fathers hath promised thee, in the land that floweth with milk and honey.

4 Hear, O Israel: the LORD our God is one LORD:

5 And thou shalt love the LORD thy God with all thine heart, and with all thy soul, and with all thy might.

6 And these words, which I command thee this day, shall be in thine heart.

7 And thou shalt teach them diligently unto thy children, and shalt talk of them when thou sittest in thine house, and when thou walkest by the way, and when thou liest down, and when thou risest up.

8 And thou shalt bind them for a sign upon thine hand, and they shall be as frontlets between thine eyes.

9 And thou shalt write them upon the posts of thy house, and on thy gates.

20 And when thy son asketh thee in time to come, saying, What mean the testimonies, and the statutes, and the judgments, which the Lord our God hath commanded you?

21 Then thou shalt say unto thy son, We were Pharaoh's bondmen in Egypt; and the Lord brought us out of Egypt with a mighty hand:

22 And the Lord shewed signs and wonders, great and sore, upon Egypt, upon Pharaoh, and upon all his household, before our eyes:

23 And he brought us out from thence, that he might bring us in, to give us the land which he sware unto our fathers.

24 And the Lord commanded us to do all these statutes, to fear the Lord our God, for our good always, that he might preserve us alive, as it is at this day.

■ **THE LESSON EXPLAINED**

Eternally Valid Teaching (6:1–3)

Having looked back at history, to teach the new generation the lessons from past failures and past blessings, Moses looked forward. He reminded the people of the basic stipulations God had for them (5:1–21). Then he prepared them to hear the rest of God's expectations (especially chs. 12–26). He made quick, clear points: commandments come from God, not man; commandments apply to life in the new land; commandments result from fear or reverence of God;

commandment obedience brings the good life, fertility, and fulfillment of the patriarchal promises.

Eternal Love for God (6:4–6)

Moses' teachings here became Israel's lifeblood. Verses 4–9 comprise Judaism's Shema (Hebrew for hear!), its basic confession of faith in God. Orthodox Jews wear them along with Exodus 13:1–16; Deuteronomy 11:13–21 in phylacteries or small black leather boxes strapped to the forehead and upper left arm. God's people must hear these words, not just with physical ears but with loving ears, a hearing bent on obeying. The words focus on the nature of God. He is one. That is, He is unique. No other being can claim to belong to the class of deity. That class has only one member. He is a whole, not divided into warring factions that are inconsistent or undecided. God is unique, reliable, and consistent. This unique nature of God has unique consequences for the people He created. Such a perfect being deserves perfect response: undivided, self-consistent love from an undivided self—intellectually, emotionally, and physically. Ideas, feelings, and actions should all reflect love of God. So never forget these words.

Eternal Duty to Teach (6:7–9)

Such good news about God—unique, self-consistent, worthy of love—must be shared. Your family needs to know. Such news is always one generation away from extinction, so teach your family. How do you teach? A one-time information session? Of course not. A daily, long-term, repetitive lifestyle, where this news about God becomes the subject of daily family conversation and action. People who see you, who visit you, who pass by your house should know you believe in and obey this God. Your identity as a God lover and God obeyer should never be in doubt for anyone.

Eternal Act of Salvation (6:20–24)

Teaching the commandments means conversing with your children. When they have questions raised by your teachings and actions, then you have answers. You can recite salvation history: God did this for us in Egypt, making us a free nation. Having saved us, He taught us the way of salvation life—a way of obedience and love expressed in His commandments. God's acts of salvation and our obedient life of salvation go together. Never one without the other!

■ TRUTHS TO LIVE BY

Relationship with God rests on consistent obedience. God has a plan and purpose for His people. He wants what is best for us. We can experience that best only as we trust Him. We trust by doing what He has asked, knowing His way is best for us. We experience God fully only as we obey Him totally.

Relationship with God continues only as you teach your children. God's people could disappear from the earth in one generation. Nothing physical such as birth or baptism guarantees that tomorrow's generation will know and serve God. Your teaching of your children lead them to keep the faith.

Relationship with God is possible because God acts to save. Our obedience does not create a relationship with God. He created the relationship by saving us through the death of Christ on the cross. We enter into the relationship He created by trusting Jesus for salvation—a trust that goes deep enough that we obey.

■ A VERSE TO REMEMBER

Hear, O Israel: the LORD our God is one LORD: And thou shalt love the LORD thy God with all thine heart, and with all thy soul, and with all thy might.—Deuteronomy 6:4, 5

■ **DAILY BIBLE READINGS**

Oct. 18 — God's Great Commandment to Israel.
Deut. 6:1–9

Oct. 19 — Do Not Follow Other Gods. Deut. 6:10–15

Oct. 20 — Tell of God's Mighty Acts. Deut. 6:16–25

Oct. 21 — Chosen by God's Love and Grace. Deut. 7:7–11

Oct. 22 — Blessing of Obedience. Deut. 10:12–22

Oct. 23 — A Land of Milk and Honey. Deut. 11:8–12

Oct. 24 — Love God and Teach Your Children.
Deut. 11:13–21

A Warning

Basic Passage: Deuteronomy 8:7–20

Forgetting is so easy. Do we deserve the freedom and power and wealth we have by living in our homeland? Or must we give thanks to heroes of the past who fought and died to give us freedom? Dare we forget the heritage of George Washington, Abraham Lincoln, Dwight D. Eisenhower, Martin Luther King Jr.? Dare we forget the pilgrims, the founders of our churches, and our own godly ancestors and parents? It seems so easy to remember what I have accomplished and so easy to forget what my parents and grandparents did that made my accomplishments possible. So Moses had to remind Israel not to forget.

▪ THE BIBLE LESSON

Deuteronomy 8

7 For the LORD thy God bringeth thee into a good land, a land of brooks of water, of fountains and depths that spring out of valleys and hills;

8 A land of wheat, and barley, and vines, and fig trees, and pomegranates; a land of olive oil, and honey;

9 A land wherein thou shalt eat bread without scarceness, thou shalt not lack any thing in it; a land whose stones are iron, and out of whose hills thou mayest dig brass.

10 When thou hast eaten and art full, then thou shalt bless the Lord thy God for the good land which he hath given thee.

11 Beware that thou forget not the Lord thy God, in not keeping his commandments, and his judgments, and his statutes, which I command thee this day:

12 Lest when thou hast eaten and art full, and hast built goodly houses, and dwelt therein;

13 And when thy herds and thy flocks multiply, and thy silver and thy gold is multiplied, and all that thou hast is multiplied;

14 Then thine heart be lifted up, and thou forget the Lord thy God, which brought thee forth out of the land of Egypt, from the house of bondage;

15 Who led thee through that great and terrible wilderness, wherein were fiery serpents, and scorpions, and drought, where there was no water; who brought thee forth water out of the rock of flint;

16 Who fed thee in the wilderness with manna, which thy fathers knew not, that he might humble thee, and that he might prove thee, to do thee good at thy latter end;

17 And thou say in thine heart, My power and the might of mine hand hath gotten me this wealth.

18 But thou shalt remember the Lord thy God: for it is he that giveth thee power to get wealth, that he may establish his covenant which he sware unto thy fathers, as it is this day.

19 And it shall be, if thou do at all forget the Lord thy God, and walk after other gods, and serve them, and worship them, I testify against you this day that ye shall surely perish.

20 As the nations which the Lord destroyeth before your face, so shall ye perish; because ye would not be obedient unto the voice of the Lord your God.

■ THE LESSON EXPLAINED

God's Good Gifts (8:7-9)

Look what's ahead. God is going to do it. The promises will be fulfilled. We will have a land of our own. We will have everything we ever dreamed of when God gets us into the land. No more of this manna and bird meat. All kinds of delicacies wait for us in the land. Just can't wait to experience all God's good gifts.

Our Forgetful Heart (8:10-17)

Just remember one thing. Don't forget, now. It is true. You will eat all those wonderful delicacies and more. The land has more for you than you can ever imagine. But how are you going to get the land? Is God going to give it to you?

What are you going to do when you enjoy the fruits of the land? Remember. Thank God for all His good gifts. How do you express such thanks? With your lips, of course. But much more. Your actions shout gratitude louder than your lips. You have and know God's expectations, His commandments. Obey them. Then you will truly say "Thank You" to God. The temptation will always haunt you: eat and forget. Build houses and forget. Get in the rut of the good life and forget. Get proud. Take credit for yourself. Forget how God made it all possible. Enjoy the good life and forget the hardships your ancestors went through with God to make this possible. God was there every minute, making this minute of the good life possible. Don't forget! Don't take credit! Don't give in to pride!

God's Promised Punishment (8:18–20)

Remember God, and what happens. Your generation becomes God's covenant people. He will be your God. You will be His people. You will love Him. He will continue to bless you. Yes, you have another option, a very real option. Forget God. Think the gods of the people now in the land are real. Think you have to serve them to get the blessings of the land. Think God got you out of Egypt and through the wilderness and into the land, but decide this God is no good for the land. You need other gods. Such thought breaks the covenant. Such thought leads to false worship. False worship leads to eternal punishment. No obedience, no land, no nation. Remember!

■ TRUTHS TO LIVE BY

What you have, God gave. Take inventory of everything you possess, every freedom you enjoy, every opportunity you have. God is the source. Remember.

What you did provided nothing. You have a lot. You can take credit for nothing. God made everything possible. He can take it all away. Remember.

What you own, God can take back. God displayed unbelievable power and love to get you all you have. Recite the list of acts God has done to bring you salvation and give you the blessings of life you have. Which of these blessings do you want to lose? God can take every one away. Remember.

■ A VERSE TO REMEMBER

Beware that thou forget not the LORD thy God, in not keeping his commandments, and his judgments, and his statutes, which I command thee this day.—Deuteronomy 8:11

■ DAILY BIBLE READINGS

Oct. 25 — Don't Let Prosperity Spoil You. Deut. 8:1–10
Oct. 26 — You Are Not Self-made People. Deut. 8:11–20
Oct. 27 — You Were a Stubborn People. Deut. 9:6–14
Oct. 28 — God Heard Moses on Your Behalf.
         Deut. 9:15–21
Oct. 29 — Moses Interceded for Israel Again.
         Deut. 9:25–29
Oct. 30 — Beware of False Prophets. Deut. 13:1–5
Oct. 31 — Purge Those Who Worship False Gods.
         Deut. 13:6–11

Joshua Succeeds Moses

Basic Passage: Deuteronomy 31:1–8; 34:5–9

Lyndon Johnson succeeding John F. Kennedy. Gerald Ford taking the oath of office to succeed Richard Nixon. Or Ronald Reagan or Bill Clinton. Which picture stands out in your mind as you remember the solemn occasions when leadership has changed hands dramatically in the history of your country? Remember the emotions that gripped your heart? Not one pure emotion, but a mixture of hope, wonder, fear, and uncertainty. Now imagine standing on the border of the Jordan River looking over into the Promised Land and realizing that faithful Moses would not take you there. You had to trust Joshua, who had never been number one man at anything. How would you feel? Did Israel's wandering people feel the same?

■ THE BIBLE LESSON

Deuteronomy 31

1 And Moses went and spake these words unto all Israel.

2 And he said unto them, I am an hundred and twenty years old this day; I can no more go out and come in: also the Lord hath said unto me, Thou shalt not go over this Jordan.

3 The Lord thy God, he will go over before thee, and he will destroy these nations from before thee, and thou shalt possess them: and Joshua, he shall go over before thee, as the Lord hath said.

4 And the Lord shall do unto them as he did to Sihon and to Og, kings of the Amorites, and unto the land of them, whom he destroyed.

5 And the Lord shall give them up before your face, that ye may do unto them according unto all the commandments which I have commanded you.

6 Be strong and of a good courage, fear not, nor be afraid of them: for the Lord thy God, he it is that doth go with thee; he will not fail thee, nor forsake thee.

7 And Moses called unto Joshua, and said unto him in the sight of all Israel, Be strong and of a good courage: for thou must go with this people unto the land which the Lord hath sworn unto their fathers to give them; and thou shalt cause them to inherit it.

8 And the Lord, he it is that doth go before thee; he will be with thee, he will not fail thee, neither forsake thee: fear not, neither be dismayed.

. . . .

Deuteronomy 34

5 So Moses the servant of the Lord died there in the land of Moab, according to the word of the Lord.

6 And he buried him in a valley in the land of Moab, over against Bethpeor: but no man knoweth of his sepulchre unto this day.

7 And Moses was an hundred and twenty years old when he died: his eye was not dim, nor his natural force abated.

8 And the children of Israel wept for Moses in the plains of Moab thirty days: so the days of weeping and mourning for Moses were ended.

9 And Joshua the son of Nun was full of the spirit of wisdom; for Moses had laid his hands upon him: and the children of Israel hearkened unto him, and did as the Lord commanded Moses.

■ THE LESSON EXPLAINED

Moses' Promise for the Future (31:1–6)

Forty years mixed with triumph and frustration! That's what Moses looked back on (compare Exod. 7:7) as he stood to address his people Israel one last time. He faced reality. His work was done. Another person would lead Israel into the land, fulfilling the hopes and dreams of Moses' forty years of labor. Could he now convince the new Israel, the generation that had never known Egypt, to enter the new land under Joshua? One major selling point supported Moses' persuasion: God is leading you and will go over with you. The question is not, Will you go with Joshua? The question is, Will you go with God? You may not know what Joshua can do. You do know what God can do. Remember what He did to Sihon and Og (see Num. 21:21–35). God promises victory. So why are you afraid? Has He ever failed you? March to victory with God!

Joshua's Commission for the Present (31:7, 8)

God goes with the people to conquer the new land. Still, human leadership is necessary. If Moses cannot go, then someone must take charge, relaying God's commands to the people as Moses had done. So Moses installed Joshua as the new leader, with the same admonition he gave the people: Do not be afraid. Have courage. Carry out God's task. Then God can accomplish His purpose. He can give you the land as your inheritance as His children. Just remember, victory does not depend on you. God goes in front of you and your army. He prepares the way. He gives the victory. He cannot fail. He must prevail. So have no fear. Let nothing upset you. Trust God. Inherit God's land.

Moses' Passing into Memory (34:5–8)

Judaism's greatest hero went the way of all people. He died. His death was not surprising. God had prepared him for it long before (Num. 20:12) when he struck the rock to get water rather than simply speaking to it as God commanded. Moses paid the penalty for his sin as all people must. Still, his death was special. He died in God's presence and had God conduct his funeral and burial—no one else. Thus, Moses became a memory for Israel, one that gave guidance to each new generation reminding them of God's expectations and God's covenant.

Interestingly, Moses did not become a memorial. God showed no one where He buried Moses, so no one could build a memorial there. Death came not through the normal processes of physical weakness. Moses still had physical power to lead. Death came at God's command, in God's way, at God's place, for God's reasons. Then the people mourned his death for a month, paying respect and homage to their leader in traditional fashion (see Num. 20:29).

Joshua's Leadership for the Future (34:9)

God has ways of preparing leaders for His people. Joshua had military experience (Exod. 17:8–16), administrative experience (Exod. 24:13; Num. 11:28), religious experience (Exod. 33:11), and minority experience (Num. 14:6). God had already elected him as Moses' successor and installed him in the position (Num. 27:18–23; compare 34:17). God gave him the one needed characteristic to lead His people: the spirit of wisdom. The spirit here is the Spirit of God (Num. 27:18). The gift of the Spirit is wisdom, that is the ability to make decisions wisely, following the leadership of the Spirit. Israel had not only a new leader; they had a new spirit. No longer was this the murmuring-in-the-wilderness generation. This generation listened to what God told Moses, obeyed Moses, and thus obeyed Joshua as Moses told them to.

■ TRUTHS TO LIVE BY

Today's leaders pass away. Human leadership is temporary. People can never confidently tie their wagon to a human star, for the light of that star soon vanishes into the grave. Trust must always be in God, not in leaders whom God raises up for the moment.

God has new leaders for tomorrow's mission. The task is never too great for God. He always has a person to lead God's people and accomplish the task. The question is always, Do God's people trust Him to give leaders, or will they select their own according to their own criteria?

God's leadership provides continuity for God's people. God appoints various human leaders to accomplish various missions. The human leader is never the constant factor. That is God's presence. God is the leader, always there where God's people are joining Him in doing His work.

■ A VERSE TO REMEMBER

And the LORD, he it is that doth go before thee; he will be with thee, he will not fail thee, neither forsake thee: fear not, neither be dismayed.—Deuteronomy 31:8

■ DAILY BIBLE READINGS

Nov. 1 — God Will Lead Israel Across Jordan.
         Deut. 31:1–6
Nov. 2 — Read and Obey the Law. Deut. 31:7–13
Nov. 3 — Joshua is Commissioned to Succeed Moses.
         Deut. 31:14–23
Nov. 4 — Death of Moses in Moab. Deut. 34:1–7
Nov. 5 — Moses Is Mourned and Remembered.
         Deut. 34:8–12
Nov. 6 — God's Promise and Command to Joshua.
         Josh. 1:1–9
Nov. 7 — Israel Prepares to Cross the Jordan.
         Josh. 1:10–16

Israel Crosses the Jordan River

Basic Passage: Joshua 3:7–17

God has led me on so many extraordinary adventures with Him. My children have never let me forget one occasion. Driving back from Germany into Switzerland after preaching at a small military church one Sunday night, we arrived at the Swiss border, less than an hour from home. Suddenly, unexpectedly, the Swiss border guards stopped the car, motioned me over to their small station, told me in no uncertain German terms to get out of the car, thrust me up against the wall of their guard hut, and began comparing my bearded face to pictures of the Bader Meinhoff terrorists pasted on their wall. My family cowered in the car waiting to see what the guards would do. Finally, they pushed me back to the car and let me travel on. I had a minor taste of the excitement and fear Israel faced as they stepped into the Jordan River to cross into their new homeland.

■ **THE BIBLE LESSON**

Joshua 3

7 And the Lord said unto Joshua, This day will I begin to magnify thee in the sight of all Israel, that they may know that, as I was with Moses, so I will be with thee.

8 And thou shalt command the priests that bear the ark of the covenant, saying, When ye are come to the brink of the water of Jordan, ye shall stand still in Jordan.

9 And Joshua said unto the children of Israel, Come hither, and hear the words of the Lord your God.

10 And Joshua said, Hereby ye shall know that the living God is among you, and that he will without fail drive out from before you the Canaanites, and the Hittites, and the Hivites, and the Perizzites, and the Girgashites, and the Amorites, and the Jebusites.

11 Behold, the ark of the covenant of the Lord of all the earth passeth over before you into Jordan.

12 Now therefore take you twelve men out of the tribes of Israel, out of every tribe a man.

13 And it shall come to pass, as soon as the soles of the feet of the priests that bear the ark of the Lord, the Lord of all the earth, shall rest in the waters of Jordan, that the waters of Jordan shall be cut off from the waters that come down from above; and they shall stand upon an heap.

14 And it came to pass, when the people removed from their tents, to pass over Jordan, and the priests bearing the ark of the covenant before the people;

15 And as they that bare the ark were come unto Jordan, and the feet of the priests that bare the ark were dipped in the brim of the water, (for Jordan overfloweth all his banks all the time of harvest,)

16 That the waters which came down from above stood and rose up upon an heap very far from the city Adam, that is beside Zaretan: and those that came down toward the sea of the plain, even the salt sea, failed, and were cut off: and the people passed over right against Jericho.

17 And the priests that bare the ark of the covenant of the Lord stood firm on dry ground in the midst of Jordan, and all the Israelites passed over on dry ground, until all the people were passed clean over Jordan.

THE LESSON EXPLAINED

Joining God's Hall of Faith (3:7–9)

God has special rewards for special leaders. He gives such leaders a special place in the heart of His people. Why? Because the leaders are more spiritual and closer to Him than the rest of the people? Hardly! He uses the leader to demonstrate His presence with the people. This places a special burden on the leader. The leader must always point the people to God's leadership, not to his own.

Joshua's leadership task was doubly tough. His assignment was to lead in the shadow of Moses. His leadership goals were accomplished only as he showed the people the continuity in God's plan, that God was still doing what He had done through Moses. So Joshua began his road to God's Hall of Faith. He heard God's directions for the priests and began to relay the message. Such absolute obedience, not individual brilliance and strategy, marks God's chosen leader.

Knowing God's Presence in Faith (3:10–13)

How does a leader prove the presence of God? Joshua faced the ultimate test. He had to get a nation of people across a raging river. He knew God's way: Walk straight into the river and depend on Me to get you through. Could he convince the people? Would they share his faith? If the people would follow this command, surely battle orders against the enemies would be simple. So Joshua laid out God's plan: Watch the ark go ahead of you, symbolizing God's presence. Remember who God is, the Master of all creation, the God who controls the entire universe. Follow the ark at the prescribed distance. When the priests carrying the ark step into the water, the flooding Jordan will suddenly split in two. You will have a dry path across the Jordan to God's new land. Do you have faith to walk into the Jordan with God?

Seeing God's Act of Deliverance in Faith (3:14–17)

It happened. The people moved out behind the ark as God commanded Joshua and as Joshua commanded the people. They could see the mighty Jordan's power. They could not know that if they waited a few months the winter snows on the northern mountains would quit melting and feeding the river, resulting in the Jordan becoming a docile trickle anyone might cross. No, they had to move at God's time, the river's flood stage. They moved. So did God. The waters divided. Look! The priests stand in the middle of mighty Jordan. The river no longer rolls. It stands still, heaped up on each side waiting for Israel to cross. So Israel crossed. Faith is rewarded. God's presence is proved. Israel has taken the first step of faith into the Promised Land.

■ TRUTHS TO LIVE BY

Faith looks to God for fame. Competition rules our world. Everyone wants to be a winner at something. Even the church too often becomes a competitive arena. We forget God's ways: fame and victory come when God metes it out. Leadership and acknowledgment come to humans only when God chooses for God's reason. Entering God's Hall of Faith means pointing others to His presence, not yours.

Faith confesses God as Lord. God's people look at the world with different eyes. The world sees tasks that are possible and tasks that are impossible. The world attempts only those tasks which seem in the realm of possibility. God leads His people to do the impossible, to cross the flooding river. His people then recognize that God was at work doing the impossible; we were not. Thus we can confess, God is Lord of all the earth. He has no rivals. He always wins. His enemies always lose.

Faith acts as God leads. The world seeks creative, energetic, charismatic leaders to motivate people to get the job done "my way." People of faith humbly look to God and carry out plans only when assured God is at work there and calling us to join Him. Until God shows Himself at work, God's people wait to act.

■ A VERSE TO REMEMBER

Be strong and of a good courage; be not afraid, neither be thou dismayed: for the LORD thy God is with thee whithersoever thou goest.—Joshua 1:9

■ DAILY BIBLE READINGS

The Destruction of Jericho

Basic Passage: Joshua 6:1–5, 15–20

Why would she do it? A beautiful young bride of a few months left her new groom, flew twenty-plus hours across the waters, and endured another ten-hour bumpy ride across African "interstates." All this so she could live two weeks in a frontier "motel" and venture forth as the only white woman among a contingent of five to ten Africans walking for six to eight hours a day among African settlements. At each settlement she spoke for five or so minutes, stopping after each sentence to let Kenyan translators relay her words first into Swahili, then into Tesso. How dare a young lady take such risks! She would retort, How dare I not. God called me to this mission trip. God helped me lead hundreds of people to faith in Him. I could do nothing else. Nothing represents an obstacle when God leads through the obstacle course.

■ **THE BIBLE LESSON.**

Joshua 6

1 Now Jericho was straitly shut up because of the children of Israel: none went out, and none came in.

2 And the Lord said unto Joshua, See, I have given into thine hand Jericho, and the king thereof, and the mighty men of valor.

3 And ye shall compass the city, all ye men of war, and go round about the city once. Thus shalt thou do six days.

4 And seven priests shall bear before the ark seven trumpets of rams' horns: and the seventh day ye shall compass the city seven times, and the priests shall blow with the trumpets.

5 And it shall come to pass, that when they make a long blast with the ram's horn, and when ye hear the sound of the trumpet, all the people shall shout with a great shout; and the wall of the city shall fall down flat, and the people shall ascend up every man straight before him.

15 And it came to pass on the seventh day, that they rose early about the dawning of the day, and compassed the city after the same manner seven times: only on that day they compassed the city seven times.

16 And it came to pass at the seventh time, when the priests blew with the trumpets, Joshua said unto the people, Shout; for the Lord hath given you the city.

17 And the city shall be accursed, even it, and all that are therein, to the Lord: only Rahab the harlot shall live, she and all that are with her in the house, because she hid the messengers that we sent.

18 And ye, in any wise keep yourselves from the accursed thing, lest ye make yourselves accursed, when ye take of the accursed thing, and make the camp of Israel a curse, and trouble it.

19 But all the silver, and gold, and vessels of brass and iron, are consecrated unto the Lord: they shall come into the treasury of the Lord.

20 So the people shouted when the priests blew with the trumpets: and it came to pass, when the people heard the sound of the trumpet, and the people shouted with a great shout, that the wall fell down flat, so that the people went up into the city, every man straight before him, and they took the city.

■ THE LESSON EXPLAINED

God's Promise to Overcome (6:1-5)

Joshua's army is coming. Shut the gates. No one can go out. No one can come in—for any reason. We are under siege. We must be prepared to wait it out, no matter how long it takes. We must repel the besiegers. Joshua cannot win this battle, for then it will propel him clear across our land. We are the first line of defense. We must stop Joshua.

Not to worry, Joshua. I have given this petty city-state into your hand. Never mind that it is the oldest walled city in the world. I have power over it, too. Just do things my way. March around the city every day for six days. Then go back to camp. Then watch me on the seventh day. Take your big signal horns. Let the priests blow them loud and clear. Then at the right moment, let the priests blow and the people shout. Jericho's walls will fall.

Human Obedience to Overcome (6:15, 16)

Strange orders. Strange battle plans. No weapons. No attacks. Just march around in circles, blow trumpets, and shout at the top of your lungs. God got us across the Jordan River because the priests obediently stepped into the flood waters. We can march in circles, blow trumpets, and shout. So they did.

Divine Warnings about Human Obstacles (6:17–19)

Obstacles of many kinds face God's people. Human enemies appear to be the greatest obstacle; they may be the least. Human pride, wanting to attack my way and not God's ways, form a more serious obstacle. God offers an even more serious obstacle. You must celebrate victory His way. These are pagan people with pagan ways. Their military might does not threaten you. Their religious might does. This one time in history you must follow the rules of "holy war." You must dedicate everything that belongs to the enemy to God. Yes, that means destroying everything—people, money, buildings, treasures. Do not leave one thing they have to contaminate you and tempt you to follow their religious patterns. Give it all to God, not to yourselves. Only one thing from Jericho joins Israel—the family of faithful, obedient Rahab (see ch. 2).

Victory over All Obstacles (6:20)

Remember God's way. March, blow, shout. There's the signal. Blow, trumpets. Shout, people. Fall, walls. Yes, just as God promised, it all happened. The world's oldest walls are flat on the ground. The city is ours. Praise God! The victory is His. No obstacles stand before God.

■ TRUTHS TO LIVE BY

God's promises overcome obstacles. God's ways appear foolish to people of the world. After all, the cross is His way of salvation, the most foolish of all foolishness according to worldly standards. Follow His foolish ways. They lead to victory over all obstacles.

God's warnings reveal obstacles. It is not as if life does not present enough obstacles to being people of God. He opens His mouth and sets forth more obstacles. We have to do things His way in victory and in celebration. Often, we do not get to enjoy the "fruits of victory." They belong to Him. We must choose anew: God's way or ours. Can our faith overcome even obstacles God seems to set in our way?

God's acts eliminate obstacles. Raising obstacles is not God's major business. Removing them is. He wants to give us peace, rest, and time to enjoy His presence. When we live life His "foolish" way, we suddenly see His victory. The world's "impossible" obstacles to success become God's toys on the way to fulfilling His purposes.

■ A VERSE TO REMEMBER

And it came to pass at the seventh time, when the priests blew with the trumpets, Joshua said unto the people, Shout; for the LORD hath given you the city.—Joshua 6:16

■ DAILY BIBLE READINGS

Nov. 15 — The Passover Celebrated at Gilgal. Josh. 5:10–15
Nov. 16 — Israel Begins Conquest of Jericho. Josh. 6:1–7
Nov. 17 — Six-Day March around Jericho's Walls.
           Josh. 6:8–14
Nov. 18 — Destruction of Jericho by Israel. Josh. 6:15–20
Nov. 19 — Rahab and Her Family Are Spared.
           Josh. 6:22–25, 27
Nov. 20 — Joshua Renews the Covenant. Josh. 8:30–35
Nov. 21 — A Sacred Song of Remembrance. Ps. 44:1–8

Choosing to Serve the Lord

Basic Passage: Joshua 24:1, 2, 14–22, 25

July 4 approaches as I write this lesson. Our president is in China seeking to improve relations with the world's most populous nation. As you teach this lesson, another patriotic holiday is on your mind—Thanksgiving. On each occasion, all over our country civic clubs, political groups, schools, and churches are planning ways to renew our allegiance and devotion to our nation. Pageants, songs, and ceremonies will display the flag, review the history, and call on us to pledge allegiance to the flag of the United States of America. Joshua reminds us of a greater allegiance, one that extends far beyond the bounds of our country to all the nations of the world for all eternity.

■ **THE BIBLE LESSON**

Joshua 24

1 And Joshua gathered all the tribes of Israel to Shechem, and called for the elders of Israel, and for their heads, and for their judges, and for their officers; and they presented themselves before God.

2 And Joshua said unto all the people, Thus saith the Lord God of Israel, Your fathers dwelt on the other side of the flood in old time, even Terah, the father of Abraham, and the father of Nachor: and they served other gods.

14 Now therefore fear the Lord, and serve him in sincerity and in truth: and put away the gods which your fathers served on the other side of the flood, and in Egypt; and serve ye the Lord.

15 And if it seem evil unto you to serve the Lord, choose you this day whom ye will serve; whether the gods which your fathers served that were on the other side of the flood, or the gods of the Amorites, in whose land ye dwell: but as for me and my house, we will serve the Lord.

16 And the people answered and said, God forbid that we should forsake the Lord, to serve other gods;

17 For the Lord our God, he it is that brought us up and our fathers out of the land of Egypt, from the house of bondage, and which did those great signs in our sight, and preserved us in all the way wherein we went, and among all the people through whom we passed:

18 And the Lord drave out from before us all the people, even the Amorites which dwelt in the land: therefore will we also serve the Lord; for he is our God.

19 And Joshua said unto the people, Ye cannot serve the Lord: for he is an holy God; he is a jealous God; he will not forgive your transgressions nor your sins.

20 If ye forsake the Lord, and serve strange gods, then he will turn and do you hurt, and consume you, after that he hath done you good.

21 And the people said unto Joshua, Nay; but we will serve the Lord.

22 And Joshua said unto the people, Ye are witnesses against yourselves that ye have chosen you the Lord, to serve him. And they said, We are witnesses.

25 So Joshua made a covenant with the people that day, and set them a statute and an ordinance in Shechem.

■ **THE LESSON EXPLAINED**

History's Bad Choices (24:1–2)

Celebrating a nation's history starts with memory, looking back at history and seeing what you learn. Often you start, like Joshua, with your nation's mistakes. Joshua gathers the people to Shechem, to Mount Ebal and Gerazim in obedience to Moses' commands (Deut. 11:26–32). Instead of instructing the priests, Joshua pulls together the leaders of life's daily activities (23:2). These leaders must enter God's presence and learn how to give religious leadership to "secular" affairs. Their first lesson is that they come from a long line of sinners. Israel's history began with Abraham (Gen. 12). Abraham's history began with his father Terah, who served other gods. Israel's history is not perfect. It is a history birthed from idolatry.

A Leader's Right Choice (24:14–18)

It is also a history plagued by those gods, so Israel faces a choice. Will they give awe, reverence, and allegiance to the God of their salvation history (vv. 3–13)? Will they serve in sincerity, more literally, "totally, perfectly"? Will they let no excuse keep them from pleasing God? Will they serve Him in truth and in faithfulness, giving allegiance to Him at all times and obeying His covenant provisions? Will they mirror in their relationship to God those qualities He has shown to them? Or will they serve the gods of the fathers, gods they have carried from the time of Abraham beyond the river in Mesopotamia, to the time of slavery in Egypt, and now to the present time with Joshua? I will give you the example. My family and I choose to serve Yahweh, the God of Israel. Your turn! What's your choice? We are with you! We choose Yahweh, too! He saved us! We choose Him.

The Impossible Choice (24:19–22)

The most shocking words in the Old Testament: You cannot serve the LORD. Why? You just invited us to and said you were going to. What do you mean by serving God? He is holy. You must be holy, morally pure and perfect. He is zealously jealous. He will not tolerate you, His first and only love, flirting with other gods. He has no automatic system of forgiveness so that you can choose half-heartedly and then come back again when it suits your pleasure. He takes seriously His covenant with you. Break the covenant and suffer the consequences. He is not like the other gods, gods you can carry around and dress up and feed. Those gods you make the rules for and you easily fulfill the rules of service. Not so with Yahweh. He makes the rules. He has shown His salvation and His faithfulness. You cannot keep the rules. He punishes those who sin. Still choose to serve Yahweh?

Yes, we still choose Yahweh. He alone deserves our worship. Yes, we know. We must bear the consequences of the choice. We will stand in court and testify against ourselves. No one made us choose Yahweh. We want to serve Him and no other gods.

Future Choices (24:25)

As God's leader for you, I accept your choice. We will make this official in this covenant we sign together in God's presence. Israel is now the people of Yahweh, pledging eternal allegiance to Him. You agree to fulfill the covenant obligations summarized in the Ten Commandments. You will be His people just as He is your God. Your future is sealed with Him.

■ TRUTHS TO LIVE BY

History does not determine your choice. We all have skeletons in our closets. No one has perfect circumstances in life. We can find ways to blame history for who we now are. God says we do not have to remain as we are. We can choose to be different in lifestyle, orientation, family faithfulness, professional goals, and in relationship to Him. Choose today. Be God's. Be different.

God deserves to be your choice. God has done everything to provide salvation and wholeness for you and your life. From creation to the Exodus to the cross to eternity, He shows His faithfulness to you. Will you be faithful to Him?

Choosing God means absolute faith. Choosing God is not a spur-of-the-moment decision to be rethought later. Choosing God is an eternal decision that means you trust Him with your entire life. You expect to devote your entire life to Him. No turning back. No second thoughts. You are His and He is yours for eternity. This is a decision of faith. You do not deserve salvation. You cannot earn it. God has given it. In joy and gratitude you choose to serve Him with all your heart, soul, and mind.

■ A VERSE TO REMEMBER

And the people said unto Joshua, The LORD our God will we serve, and his voice will we obey.—Joshua 24:24

■ DAILY BIBLE READINGS

Nov. 22 — Joshua Summons Israel to Remember God. Josh. 23:1–5

Nov. 23 — Israel Exhorted to Love and Obey God. Josh. 23:6–13

Nov. 24 — Joshua Warns Against Unfaithfulness to God. Josh. 23:15–16

Nov. 25 — Joshua Rehearses Israel's History. Josh. 24:1–7

Nov. 26 — Israel Promises to Be Faithful. Josh. 24:14–18

Nov. 27 — Israel Renews the Covenant. Josh. 24:19–24

Nov. 28 — Death of Joshua and Eleazar. Josh. 24:25–31

King's Herald and Baptism

Basic Passage: Matthew 3:1–8, 11–17

Who is Jesus? This is the most important question you will ever hear. It is the most important question you will ever answer. The next thirteen weeks you will face this question every time you study God's Word, for we are entering Matthew's Gospel. Matthew, one of Christ's twelve apostles, pictures his Lord as the one who truly fulfills Israel's history, truly teaches the meaning of Moses' covenant law, truly provides eternal salvation, and truly reigns as King of Israel and King of all nations. Matthew asks you, *Is Jesus King of your life?*

■ THE BIBLE LESSON

Matthew 3

1 In those days came John the Baptist, preaching in the wilderness of Judaea,

2 And saying, Repent ye: for the kingdom of heaven is at hand.

3 For this is he that was spoken of by the prophet Esaias, saying, The voice of one crying in the wilderness, Prepare ye the way of the Lord, make his paths straight.

4 And the same John had his raiment of camel's hair, and a leathern girdle about his loins; and his meat was locusts and wild honey.

5 Then went out to him Jerusalem, and all Judaea, and all the region round about Jordan,

6 And were baptized of him in Jordan, confessing their sins.

7 But when he saw many of the Pharisees and Sadducees come to his baptism, he said unto them, O generation of vipers, who hath warned you to flee from the wrath to come?

8 Bring forth therefore fruits meet for repentance:

11 I indeed baptize you with water unto repentance: but he that cometh after me is mightier than I, whose shoes I am not worthy to bear: he shall baptize you with the Holy Ghost, and with fire:

12 Whose fan is in his hand, and he will thoroughly purge his floor, and gather his wheat into the garner; but he will burn up the chaff with unquenchable fire.

13 Then cometh Jesus from Galilee to Jordan unto John, to be baptized of him.

14 But John forbad him, saying, I have need to be baptized of thee, and comest thou to me?

15 And Jesus answering said unto him, Suffer it to be so now: for thus it becometh us to fulfill all righteousness. Then he suffered him.

16 And Jesus, when he was baptized, went up straightway out of the water: and, lo, the heavens were opened unto him, and he saw the Spirit of God descending like a dove, and lighting upon him:

17 And lo a voice from heaven, saying, This is my beloved Son, in whom I am well pleased.

■ THE LESSON EXPLAINED

Repentance as Kingdom Preparation (3:1–4)

Abruptly John the Baptist enters the scene of Matthew's Gospel without introduction or preparation. Rudely, he demands: Repent, the kingdom of heaven is at hand. You have to look up and see who this unexpected preacher is. What a shock! He claims to fulfill God's prophecy of the one who would prepare the way for Messiah to come (see Isa. 40:3). We haven't had a prophet for four hundred years, since Malachi. Why should one appear now? He wears strange clothes. Seems to be trying to look like that old prophet Elijah (2 Kings 1:8; compare Zech. 13:4). He is the sign that God's kingdom is just around the corner? He wants us to go to him and repent? His way of life is more godly than ours? What is happening here?

Baptism as Kingdom Preparation (3:5–8)

A new voice in the wilderness attracts crowds. No one has ever seen anyone like this. People are willing to walk miles and miles just to see what is going on. Once they see, something happens. They believe what this man says. The people of Israel are not in right relationship with God. They need to confess their sins. They need to turn away from the life they are living to a life dedicated to God and His will. They are willing to let John put them under water, baptize them in the dirty Jordan River, to symbolize to all the world what has happened in their hearts. They are willing publicly to say, I am a sinner who needs a new way of life. I want to be part of God's kingdom.

Even the religious leaders, people who do not get along well and who dispute nearly every religious question with one another, come together to hear John. What a reaction. John calls them a bunch of snakes and says they face God's eternal wrath. He demands more than baptism and confession of sin from them. He wants concrete action that shows they have changed their way of life.

The Spirit as Kingdom Preparation (3:11–17)

Remember, people, as I baptize you. This is only preparation. The real thing comes later. I prepare the way. The Messiah is coming. I do not measure up to Him in any way. I do not even deserve to stoop down and take off His shoes and carry them for Him like a slave would. I baptize with water for repentance. He will baptize you so that you receive the Holy Spirit. This Spirit like a flame of fire will enter your life and burn away anything unholy which would prevent the Spirit from living in your life. That same Spirit will bring fire of judgment on those who refuse to repent. Yes, the coming Messiah comes in judgment. He will bring God's people together as His harvest and burn all the rest up as useless chaff.

Here is the next candidate for John's baptism. Why, it is Jesus. You cannot be baptized. You are the coming One. You need to baptize me.

No. Go ahead and baptize Me. I must do everything expected of every other person to be part of God's kingdom. I do not want to miss one single step. So John baptized Jesus. Jesus looked up and saw God's Spirit coming to Him like a dove floating down on the breezes of heaven. A voice said: This is my Son. I love Him. I am delighted in what He is doing.

The Spirit has come. The heavens have spoken. Is the kingdom of God here? Have you repented and been baptized?

■ TRUTHS TO LIVE BY

Repentance is the first step to the kingdom.
Holy God cannot live amid unholy people. You must change your way of living. This starts with admitting you are living in sin. You decide to change and not live in sin. You ask God to guide you to live in His ways. You repent.

Baptism reflects your decision to enter the kingdom. Repentance is a private act between you and your God. The kingdom is the public power of God at work in the world. To be part of the kingdom, you participate in a public act. You let the world know you have died to an old way of sinful life and have risen to a new kind of godly life. You are baptized in public to confess your faith in God.

The Spirit affirms your place in the kingdom. Just as the Spirit came to Jesus when He was baptized, so the Spirit of God comes to take control of your life when you confess your sins and follow God in believer's baptism. Experiencing the Spirit directing your life, you know you are a part of the kingdom. You are the Spirit's person.

■ A VERSE TO REMEMBER

I indeed baptize you with water unto repentance: but he that cometh after me is mightier than I, whose shoes I am not worthy to bear: he shall baptize you with the Holy Ghost, and with fire.—Matthew 3:11

■ DAILY BIBLE READINGS

Nov. 29 — John Preaches and Baptizes. Matt. 3:1–6
Nov. 30 — John Proclaims Jesus' Coming. Matt. 3:7–12
Dec. 1 — Jesus Is Baptized by John. Matt. 3:13–17
Dec. 2 — John Sends Messengers to Question Jesus. Matt. 11:2–6
Dec. 3 — Jesus Praises John the Baptist. Matt. 11:7–11
Dec. 4 — Jesus Admonishes the Crowd. Matt. 11:12–19
Dec. 5 — John the Baptist Is Executed. Matt. 14:1–12

Temptations and Ministry

Basic Passage: Matthew 4:1–14

A single man in a married world. A stranger in a new city where residents for thirty years somehow are not yet full citizens of a community dominated by three- or four-generation families. An experienced teacher in a new church with no one to teach. Life has certainly changed in the last two years. Changes have brought something predictable but unexpected: changed temptations. The new style of life forced on me by new changes shouts out to accept self-pity, loneliness, lack of ministry, feelings of worthlessness, inertia, and other strange feelings and longings as natural and to be expected in this new world. Daily, I must rise and find new strength and new Presence to overcome temptation and find God's lifestyle, God's emotions, God's identity for me for that new day.

■ THE BIBLE LESSON

Matthew 4

1 Then was Jesus led up of the spirit into the wilderness to be tempted of the devil.

2 And when he had fasted forty days and forty nights, he was afterward an hungered.

3 And when the tempter came to him, he said, If thou be the Son of God, command that these stones be made bread.

4 But he answered and said, It is written, Man shall not live by bread alone, but by every word that proceedeth out of the mouth of God.

5 Then the devil taketh him up into the holy city, and setteth him on a pinnacle of the temple,

6 And saith unto him, If thou be the Son of God, cast thyself down: for it is written, He shall give his angels charge concerning thee: and in their hands they shall bear thee up, lest at any time thou dash thy foot against a stone.

7 Jesus said unto him, It is written again, Thou shalt not tempt the Lord thy God.

8 Again, the devil taketh him up into an exceeding high mountain, and sheweth him all the kingdoms of the world, and the glory of them;

9 And saith unto him, All these things will I give thee, if thou wilt fall down and worship me.

10 Then saith Jesus unto him, Get thee hence, Satan: for it is written, Thou shalt worship the Lord thy God, and him only shalt thou serve.

11 Then the devil leaveth him, and, behold, angels came and ministered unto him.

12 Now when Jesus had heard that John was cast into prison, he departed into Galilee;

13 And leaving Nazareth, he came and dwelt in Capernaum, which is upon the sea coast, in the borders of Zabulon and Nephthalim:

14 That it might be fulfilled which was spoken by Esaias the prophet.

■ THE LESSON EXPLAINED

The Spirit Leads to the Devil's Test (4:1, 2)

Jesus had to face life in all its parts, the good and the bad. He followed the Spirit of God into each part. Yes, the Spirit led to the difficult parts of life just as to the more enjoyable parts. Thus it surprises us, but shouldn't, as we read that the Spirit led Jesus into the wilderness to the devil to be tempted.

How did Jesus prepare for temptation? He gave up eating. Spent forty days and nights without food, at least without physical food. Certainly, the time not eating was spent praying, feasting on spiritual food for the ordeal ahead.

The Christ Uses Scripture to Answer Satan's Tests (4:3–11)

The tempter knows how to hit us where it hurts. Forty days without food. Here, Jesus, make some. Surely the Son of God can do a simple thing like turn rocks to bread.

Look at the Scrolls. Deuteronomy 8:3 tells us we have more nourishment than bread. We have God's Word to obey.

I know Scripture, too. Psalm 91:11, 12 promises angelic protection for Messiah. Prove that's who You are. Come with me to Jerusalem. Climb up to the highest part of the temple where everyone can see You. Now, jump down. Let the angels catch You, and the city will catch the vision of who You are.

Deuteronomy 6:16 says not to tempt God. I refuse to do so. God has a way for Me to be Messiah and save the world. His way does not lead to the top of the temple so angels can dramatically rescue Me from a foolish act.

God's purpose is for You to save the world. Come with me. Here we are on the highest mountain in sight. Look at the world spread at Your feet—most magnificent sight imaginable. It can all be Yours. Then You will fulfill Your mission quickly. Just fall down and worship me one time. The world is Yours.

Scat, Satan. Look at Deuteronomy 6:13 and 10:20. I am to worship God and no one else. So Satan left, replaced by God's ministering angels. The Son of God become man had endured the major temptations humans face—focusing on physical needs, testing God's saving power in foolish ways, serving the devil to achieve heavenly purposes. The Son of Man distinguished Himself from all other human beings. He did not fall for a single one of Satan's tricks. He was tempted, but did not sin (Heb. 4:15).

Fulfilling Scripture in a Time of Testing (4:12–14)

Testing time was not over. Herod stood as Satan's political representative. He threw John into prison. Could the one John pointed to be far behind? So Jesus moved from the insignificant village of Nazareth to the commercial center of Capernaum. Why? Hiding in the city from Herod? Of course not! Fulfilling Isaiah 9:1? Certainly! Testing time is always Scripture reading and Scripture obeying time.

■ TRUTHS TO LIVE BY

Testing is a part of God's plan. God wants faith to grow and dedication to Him to increase. Such cannot happen if a person has no choices to make. Satan puts choices in our way, but we can choose God's way and in so doing become more like God.

Scripture gives the answers to Satan's tests. God does not leave us without direction in testing time. We mature by fellowshiping with Him in His Word. Then when we face tests, we recall His Word that points us to the right answer for Satan's wiles.

Passing Satan's tests gives opportunity for God's ministry. Obedience to God is experience of God. As we experience God, He shows us where He is at work and invites us to join in. We may have to move to another locale or change profession, but we have the maturity of faith to follow where He leads in His work.

■ A VERSE TO REMEMBER

Then saith Jesus unto him, Get thee hence, Satan: for it is written, Thou shalt worship the Lord thy God, and him only shalt thou serve.—Matthew 4:10

■ DAILY BIBLE READINGS

Dec. 6   — Jesus Is Tempted by the Devil. Matt. 4:1–11

Birth of Jesus

Basic Passage: Matthew 1:1–6, 18–25

Christmas! What a wonderful time of year. Parties with friends and family. Special worship services. Giving and receiving gifts. Oh, the joys of Christmas! Unless you are alone! Christmas is also the leading season for suicide in our nation. Why? Because it raises such high expectations that it makes failure to achieve such happy expectations seem reason for ending it all. Another look at the Christmas story points us in another direction. The first Christmas began as the loneliest, darkest moment in life for the key figures of Christmas.

■ THE BIBLE LESSON

Matthew 1

1 The book of the generation of Jesus Christ, the son of David, the son of Abraham.

2 Abraham begat Isaac; and Isaac begat Jacob; and Jacob begat Judas and his brethren;

3 And Judas begat Phares and Zara of Thamar; and Phares begat Esrom; and Esrom begat Aram;

4 And Aram begat Aminadab; and Aminadab begat Naasson; and Naasson begat Salmon;

5 And Salmon begat Booz of Rachab; and Booz begat Obed of Ruth; and Obed begat Jesse;

6 And Jesse begat David the king; and David the king begat Solomon of her that had been the wife of Urias;

18 Now the birth of Jesus Christ was on this wise: When as his mother Mary was espoused to Joseph, before they came together, she was found with child of the Holy Ghost.

19 Then Joseph her husband, being a just man, and not willing to make her a publick example, was minded to put her away privily.

20 But while he thought on these things, behold, the angel of the Lord appeared unto him in a dream, saying, Joseph, thou son of David, fear not to take unto thee Mary thy wife: for that which is conceived in her is of the Holy Ghost.

21 And she shall bring forth a son, and thou shalt call his name JESUS: for he shall save his people from their sins.

22 Now all this was done, that it might be fulfilled which was spoken of the Lord by the prophet, saying,

23 Behold, a virgin shall be with child, and shall bring forth a son, and they shall call his name Emmanuel, which being interpreted is, God with us.

24 Then Joseph being raised from sleep did as the angel of the Lord had bidden him, and took unto him his wife:

25 And knew her not till she had brought forth her first-born son: and he called his name JESUS.

■ THE LESSON EXPLAINED

The Son of David (1:1-6)

Roots analysis continues to fascinate and occupy people. They seek to know who they are by finding from whom they came. Matthew makes clear Jesus' roots. He came from David and Abraham. Not to say it was a perfect lineage. The sexual machinations of Tamar and Judah (Gen. 38) and of David and Bathsheba (2 Sam. 11, 12) are involved. The deceptions of Jacob and his mother helped pave the way (Gen. 27). The foreigner Ruth did her part (Ruth 1-4). So many ancestors, each with good and bad stories to tell, led to Jesus, who came to fulfill the promises to David (2 Sam. 7).

The Virgin Son of God (1:18-20)

What a shocking surprise. Pious, kind Joseph making final wedding plans with his Mary, already committed to be his through the rite of engagement. Then he learns: Mary's expecting. What to do? He loved her too much to follow the letter of the law and stone her (Lev. 20:10; Deut. 22:22). He would take the fairer way out. He would simply divorce her (see Deut. 24:1). Then God intervened. His angelic messenger had another path for Joseph—to marry Mary. Becoming the child's father was unique and special. No human father involved, only the Holy Spirit. Mary had not deceived Joseph. She remained a pure virgin, if a pregnant one. This was God's doing, fulfilling Isaiah 7:14. Do it God's way.

The Savior from Sins (1:21, 22)

Mary's Son was special. God had a special name for Him, Jesus, coming from the Hebrew Joshua, and meaning "Yahweh saves." Jesus would save not from military armies as Joshua did, but from sin; not for a while until the next battle, but for eternity.

The Man Who Is God With Us (1:23–25)

Yes, Jesus' birth fulfilled Isaiah 7:14, a virgin-born child. It fulfilled the second half of the verse, too: a Son called Immanuel, God with Us. Jesus was the human son of Mary. He was also the divine Son of God. Look at Jesus, and you see God at work bringing in His kingdom. Now Joseph had no choice. No stoning. No divorce. Simple obedience to God. Marry Mary. No relations with her until the child was born. Then normal marriage with a unique Son, Jesus, Son of David, Son of God, Son of Mary, Savior from sins, God with Us.

■ TRUTHS TO LIVE BY

Rejoice, for Scripture is fulfilled. Everything about Jesus' birth was unique, for His birth capped God's work from creation until that very mysterious, wonderful moment of a baby's birth. All God did and said in the Old Testament found its goal and purpose in Jesus. God is faithful. He did what He promised. Hallelujah!

Rejoice, for your sins are forgiven. Jesus is the Savior God sent. He went from Bethlehem's stable birthward to Calvary's cross death. He did it all because He loved you and wanted you to have eternal life inspite of your sins. Hallelujah!

Rejoice, for God is with us. Jesus was God in flesh. He shows you beyond a shadow of a doubt that the Creator of the universe has not fled for parts unknown. God is still here in person caring for His creation and providing salvation for His sinful people. Come, see Jesus and experience God. Hallelujah!

■ A VERSE TO REMEMBER

And she shall bring forth a son, and thou shalt call his name JESUS: for he shall save his people from their sins.—Matthew 1:21

■ DAILY BIBLE READINGS

Dec. 13 — The Genealogy of Jesus the Messiah.
        Matt. 1:1–11
Dec. 14 — Jesus' Genealogy Completed. Matt. 1:12–17
Dec. 15 — The Birth of Jesus the Messiah. Matt. 1:18–25
Dec. 16 — The Angel Gabriel Visits Mary. Luke 1:26–38
Dec. 17 — Mary Visits Her Cousin Elizabeth.
        Luke 1:39–45
Dec. 18 — Mary's Song of Praise. Luke 1:46–56
Dec. 19 — The Eternal Origin of Jesus. John 1:1–14

Coming of the Wise Men

Basic Passage: Matthew 2:1-12

It's a long strange instrument. The body looks like a long, extended hippopotamus. It's neck reaches up to the sky like a giraffe's. Strings reach from neck to body, creating an original form like the harp. The body is hollow, inviting someone to beat it like a drum. So two people play it at the same time, one on strings, the other on drums. Kenyan Christians carry this wonderful blue and white instrument across the country on bicycle, or simply walking, so that churches for miles around can worship with traditional tribal music.

I have worshiped God in the skyscraping cathedrals of Europe, in the million-dollar acoustically perfect worship houses of America, and in the open-country traditional red brick churches of the rural South. Nowhere have I been closer to God than joining with my black friends in Kenya as they lifted praise on ancient instruments and brought live animals, bolts of cloth, and stalks of grain down the aisle as their offerings.

■ THE BIBLE LESSON

Matthew 2

1 Now when Jesus was born in Bethlehem of Judaea in the days of Herod the king, behold, there came wise men from the east to Jerusalem,

2 Saying, Where is he that is born King of the Jews? For we have seen his star in the east, and are come to worship him.

3 When Herod the king had heard these things, he was troubled, and all Jerusalem with him.

4 And when he had gathered all the chief priests and scribes of the people together, he demanded of them where Christ should be born.

5 And they said unto him, In Bethlehem of Judaea: for thus it is written by the prophet,

6 And thou Bethlehem, in the land of Juda, art not the least among the princes of Juda: for out of thee shall come a Governor, that shall rule my people Israel.

7 Then Herod, when he had privily called the wise men, inquired of them diligently what time the star appeared.

8 And he sent them to Bethlehem, and said, Go and search diligently for the young child; and when ye have found him, bring me word again, that I may come and worship him also.

9 When they had heard the king, they departed; and, lo, the star, which they saw in the east, went before them, till it came and stood over where the young child was.

10 When they saw the star, they rejoiced with exceeding great joy.

11 And when they were come into the house, they saw the young child with Mary his mother, and fell down, and worshiped him: and when they had opened their treasures, they presented unto him gifts; gold, and frankincense, and myrrh.

12 And being warned of God in a dream that they should not return to Herod, they departed into their own country another way.

■ THE LESSON EXPLAINED

True Worship (2:1–2)

Mark begins his Gospel with John the Baptist's ministry. John begins with the birth of creation before skipping to the confession of John. Luke takes great pains to describe the parallel births of John and Jesus. Matthew starts with genealogy, connecting Jesus to the promises of God to Abraham and David, presents Joseph's dilemma over Mary's pregnancy, highlights the prophetic background for Jesus' birth, mentions Joseph's obedient naming of the baby, and then focuses on the great visitation—educated counselors of mysterious eastern kings following a star to find the new King of the Jews. Such is true worship, leaving responsibilities, family, possessions . . . everything to determine where God is mysteriously at work and join Him.

False Worship (2:3–8)

Foreign counselors left their pagan astrology charts and divination instruments to find the true King. The ruling king of the Jews left all government business and functions to gather his religious advisers to consult Scriptures. Surely, he is more on the right track of worship than pagan sages. He has God's holy Word and God's ordained priests and teachers. They have only an isolated star in the sky. His counselors take only minutes to find Micah 5:2 and see that the Messiah comes from Bethlehem, the city of David's birth, where God is to grow a new branch from the stump of Jesse's family tree.

The foreigners take months to follow a star through the desolate wilderness and must still stop and ask Herod the way. Hearing of Bethlehem, the wise counselors are gratefully satisfied, ready to go on their way. The king of the Jews is greedily demanding of more information. When did the star appear? How long has it been? That is, how old must the child be? Then he releases them to Bethlehem to find the child and report his whereabouts back to him. To worship, he says. Later actions speak much more loudly. To kill, they say. His worship is devoted to himself and his position, not to the child at the end of the star.

Generous Worship (2:9–12)

King Herod's false worship is ready to take all and give nothing. The foreign king's advisors faithfully follow the star to God's destination. Unspeakable joy thrills their souls. First glance of the child sends them to their knees in adoration and praise. Saddlebags come open for the first time on the long journey. Carefully sequestered gifts come out—gold: the most precious of metals for buying power; frankincense: expensive incense and perfume from southern Arabia central to Jewish worship (Exod. 30:34; Lev. 2:1, 2; 24:7); and myrrh: sweet-smelling resin from South Arabia used in anointing oil (Exod. 30:23), as perfume (Esther 2:12); for deodorizing (Ps. 45:8), and in embalming the dead (John 19:39).

Yes, foreign kings spared no expense to honor and worship the child. The Jewish king spared no energy in seeking His death. God honored the representatives of the world in their true worship by showing them where to go. He foiled the attempts of the Jewish king to protect his own power.

■ TRUTHS TO LIVE BY

Worship requires your time and energy. Wise men left home on a long, tiresome journey to give homage to one they did not know. Too often we spend worship time watching our watches to see when we can do something else.

Worship is God-serving, not self-serving. The wise men abandoned their position to find Jesus. Herod sought to find Jesus to protect his position and power. God honored those who forgot their own importance. Worship is time and energy dedicated totally to God with no thought of oneself.

Worship requires your possessions. Herod gave nothing and wanted to gain everything. The wise men gave everything with no thought of gaining anything. Worship is not simply a specified time on the calendar. Worship is the dedication and sacrifice of every resource you have for the good of God's kingdom.

■ A VERSE TO REMEMBER

Where is he that is born King of the Jews? for we have seen his star in the east, and are come to worship him.—Matthew 2:2

■ DAILY BIBLE READINGS

Dec. 20 — The Birth of Jesus. Luke 2:1–7

The Twelve Disciples

Basic Passage: Matthew 4:18–22; 9:9–12; 10:1–4

Samson A. Kisia, Amos Osakiha, Hannington Wilberforce, Magero Charles, Opemi Oayho . . . the list goes on and on. These are disciples of Jesus walking or riding on bicycles through the dirt paths of Kenya amid unspeakable disease to tell people of the Savior who loves them. It may well be that if Jesus came today to search out twelve apostles for his mission work, He would go first to Kenya, where young Patrick was willing to travel more than twenty miles a day for eight days on a bicycle just for the privilege of translating for me as I tried to share Jesus with his people. Apostolic commitment means taking up one's cross ready to die for Jesus. This I see daily in Kenya, but so seldom here. Why?

■ THE BIBLE LESSON

Matthew 4

18 And Jesus walking by the sea of Galilee, saw two brethren, Simon called Peter, and Andrew his brother, casting a net into the sea: for they were fishers.

19 And he saith unto them, Follow me, and I will make you fishers of men.

20 And they straightway left their nets, and followed him.

21 And going on from thence, he saw other two brethren, James the son of Zebedee, and John his brother, in a ship with Zebedee their father, mending their nets; and he called them.

22 And they immediately left the ship and their father, and followed him.

. . . .

Matthew 9

9 And as Jesus passed forth from thence, he saw a man, named Matthew, sitting at the receipt of custom: and he saith unto him, Follow me. And he arose, and followed him.

10 And it came to pass, as Jesus sat at meat in the house, behold, many publicans and sinners came and sat down with him and his disciples.

11 And when the Pharisees saw it, they said unto his disciples, Why eateth your Master with publicans and sinners?

12 But when Jesus heard that, he said unto them, They that be whole need not a physician, but they that are sick.

. . . .

Matthew 10

1 And when he had called unto him his twelve disciples, he gave them power against unclean spirits, to cast them out, and to heal all manner of sickness and all manner of disease.

2 Now the names of the twelve apostles are these; The first, Simon, who is called Peter, and Andrew his brother; James the son of Zebedee, and John his brother;

3 Philip, and Bartholomew; Thomas, and Matthew the publican; James the son of Alphaeus, and Lebbaeus, whose surname was Thaddaeus;

4 Simon the Canaanite, and Judas Iscariot, who also betrayed him.

■ THE LESSON EXPLAINED

Fishers of Men (4:18–22)

Minding our own business, just trying to make a living for our families. Then this wandering teacher appears. Come, go with Me, He said. Leave your fishing nets and enter a new business. Fish for men. Ridiculous request. What would we tell our families? How would they eat? Why would we want to give up this comfortable routine and go with this man? You know what. We did it. We threw down our nets and went with Jesus, just like that. Why? No explanation. He called. We could do nothing but obey. That is who He is. Know what else? We were not the only ones. He went a little further and found James and John. They did the same thing we did. You figure it.

Healers of Sinners (9:9–12)

What a situation I found myself in. A Jew working for the enemy, yes, working for the Roman government. Not only working for them, but taking taxes from my own people to pay to them. Can't explain how or why I got into the situation, but there I was. Then He came. Follow Me, He commanded. Now that was a choice. Go from certain financial success to no income at all. Go from working for the Romans to following One some people said would be the new King of the Jews, overthrowing the Romans. Choice seemed simple enough. Always choose financial security. I always had, but not this time. I got up and followed. Why? He said to.

First stop, a party with all the other tax collectors in the region. Never been a party like this, a Jewish rabbi, teacher of God's Word, associating with these ritually impure, political outcasts from Judaism. There was Jesus. There I was. Of course, this was just what the Pharisees wanted, a chance to accuse Jesus of breaking the law. What an answer He gave. Who needs a doctor? The sick or the well? He implied that the Pharisees never helped the ones in need. That's the only people we ever seemed to deal with.

Power over Spirits (10:1–4)

What a bunch Jesus chose! Two sets of fishermen brothers—Peter and Andrew, James and John; then Philip, always leading people to Jesus and asking questions (John 1:43–51; 6:5–7; 12:21, 22; 14:8, 9); mysterious Bartholomew, always present in the lists of disciples but never active; probably Philip's brother Nathaniel (John 1:43–51); doubting Thomas needing proof but he was loyal and courageous (John 11:16; 20:24–25); Matthew the renegade tax collector turned Gospel author also called Levi (Matt. 9:9; Mark 2:14; Luke 5:27); James the son of Alphaeus, probably outshone by his mother, who accompanied Jesus to the cross (Matt. 27:56; Mark 15:40; 16:2; Luke 24:10); Lebbaeus, also known as Thaddaeus or Judas not Iscariot, noted only for one vital question (John 14:22); Simon, better known for his associations with Canaanites and Zealots, thus one with a radical fringe heritage (Luke 6:15). Finally, there was Judas, the traitor and treasurer. What a group. Only Jesus could combine them into a force that could cast out demonic spirits and create the church that would spread to the ends of the earth.

■ TRUTHS TO LIVE BY

Commitment to Jesus means to seek converts to Him. Jesus calls us to follow and to invite others to follow, too. Have you invited someone to know Jesus this week? Why not?

Commitment to Jesus means to accept sinners, not sin. Jesus' favorite hangouts were places where sinners gathered. He never imitated them, simply expressed concern over their condition and helped heal their spiritual illnesses.

Commitment to Jesus means to exercise God's power. Are you uncomfortable with this? So were the disciples at first, but the One with all power from heaven shares that power with those who follow Him. Weakness in your life is an indication you have taken a vacation from Jesus.

■ A VERSE TO REMEMBER

Follow me, and I will make you fishers of men. —Matthew 4:19

■ DAILY BIBLE READINGS

Dec. 27 — Jesus Calls the First Disciples. Matt. 4:18–22
Dec. 28 — Jesus Calls Matthew. Matt. 9:9–13
Dec. 29 — Authority Conferred Upon the Disciples.
          Matt. 10:1–4
Dec. 30 — The Twelve Proclaim God's Kingdom. Matt. 10:5–15
Dec. 31 — Disciples Told of Coming Persecutions.
          Matt. 10:16–25
Jan. 1 — The Disciples Told Not to Fear. Matt. 10:26–33
Jan. 2 — Not Peace but a Sword. Matt. 10:34–11:1

Teachings on Prayer

Basic Passage: Matthew 6:1–15

Samson is named for a giant, but he's not very big. At least, physically he's not very big. Spiritually, that's another matter. Samson leads Kenyan Baptists. Last summer as I watched him take our crew of white volunteers into parts of Kenya full-time missionaries never entered, I found how Samson leads. He leads from his knees. He talks to God expectantly. He tells God what needs to be done in Kenya. Samson is so close to God's heart that he knows what needs to be done in Kenya. He asks God to let exactly what needs to be done be done. And it is so. God answers Samson's unreasonable prayers. Miracles happen. Supplies appear. People volunteer. From out of nowhere land for churches is donated by people with no connection to any church. Samson does not have to preach and teach the power of prayer. He practices it.

■ THE BIBLE LESSON

Matthew 6

1 Take heed that ye do not your alms before men, to be seen of them: otherwise ye have no reward of your Father which is in heaven.

2 Therefore when thou doest thine alms, do not sound a trumpet before thee, as the hypocrites do in the synagogues and in the streets, that they may have glory of men. Verily I say unto you, They have their reward.

3 But when thou doest alms, let not thy left hand know what thy right hand doeth:

4 That thine alms may be in secret: and thy Father which seeth in secret himself shall reward thee openly.

5 And when thou prayest, thou shalt not be as the hypocrites are: for they love to pray standing in the synagogues and in the corners of the streets, that they may be seen of men. Verily I say unto you, They have their reward.

6 But thou, when thou prayest, enter into thy closet, and when thou hast shut thy door, pray to thy Father which is in secret; and thy Father which seeth in secret shall reward thee openly.

7 But when ye pray, use not vain repetitions, as the heathen do: for they think that they shall be heard for their much speaking.

8 Be not ye therefore like unto them: for your Father knoweth what things ye have need of, before ye ask him.

9 After this manner therefore pray ye: Our Father which art in heaven, Hallowed be thy name.

10 Thy kingdom come. Thy will be done in earth, as it is in heaven.

11 Give us this day our daily bread.

12 And forgive us our debts, as we forgive our debtors.

13 And lead us not into temptation, but deliver us from evil: For thine is the kingdom, and the power, and the glory, for ever. Amen.

14 For if ye forgive men their trespasses, your heavenly Father will also forgive you:

15 But if ye forgive not men their trespasses, neither will your Father forgive your trespasses.

■ THE LESSON EXPLAINED

Secret Practice (6:1–6)

Jesus taught in context. In His day, you knew the people who were really religious. They made sure you saw and heard their religion as they told others how to live and found the important street corners to show others how they prayed. Jesus would have none of that. They tooted their own horns quite loudly. Giving money to the temple? Right time, right place: everyone around watching. Send the coins into the metal collection urn at just the right angle so they resounded all the way down. Everyone knew they gave a lot.

Jesus turned the practice upside down. One-handed drop into the urn, all the way to the bottom without touching anything. No one hears a sound. Your left hand does not know how much the right one put in. But God knows. That's all that matters. Same way with prayer. Pick up all your fancy prayer blankets and prayer shawls. Get off the street corner into the prayer corner of your house. Talk to God with no one else listening in. God hears. God answers. Nothing else matters.

Sincere Procedure (6:7, 8)

Simple place. Simple words. Say what your heart feels and shut up. You do not have to repeat yourself. God hears the first time, and no one else is listening in at your prayer closet. God does not count the number of words. He counts only the relationship you have with Him. He does not really need to hear what you say. He already knows. The experience teaches you to depend on Him, not on the opinion or actions of other people.

Selfless Purpose (6:9–15)

Prayer has basic components for a basic purpose. Jesus taught these just as simply as the procedure He taught in prayer. No repetition. No big words. Nothing to impress others. Just a way to share with God the deepest feelings and desires of your heart and those of your worshiping community, for the prayers are stated in plural, not singular.

Acknowledge who God is, the heavenly Father, close as your daddy but above and beyond all that is human. Show your relationship to Him, a sinner on earth confessing the holy purity of God and wanting all the world to see what you have experienced of God's perfection.

Pray for the future: a new heaven and new earth where God is king, acknowledged and served by all so that His will, not human greed, is fulfilled every minute. Pray for the present: provision of basic human need, forgiveness of personal wrong, and a change of heart that makes you as forgiving as you want God to be.

Pray for daily problems: decision making pleasing to God and not to Satan; opportunities to witness to the power and presence of God's kingdom, His power, and His honor rather than your own.

Remember, all prayer hinges on your attitude. You are giving, not getting; forgiving, not condemning; dependent on God, not on your own power of vengeance. Only the forgiver can pray.

■ TRUTHS TO LIVE BY

Prayer is a personal relationship, not a public proclamation. Prayer is cementing your trust in and dependence on God and experiencing His love and guidance for your life. Prayer is a two-party connection; no third party is ever needed.

Prayer trusts an all-knowing God. Prayer is positioning yourself before God as one who needs forgiveness, is forgiving of others, and understands that God knows best. Prayer demonstrates your trust more than your knowledge of what is needed.

Prayer depends on God and forgives people. People are the beneficiaries of your prayer life, not the participants. Because you trust, love, and obey God, you relate to other people in trust and love. Prayer lets you see your own weakness and frees you to let others be as imperfect as you are. Prayer shows you have to have forgiveness to live with God, so you respond in forgiveness to others, imitating the way God responds to you.

■ A VERSE TO REMEMBER

But thou, when thou prayest, enter into thy closet, and when thou hast shut thy door, pray to thy Father which is in secret; and thy Father which seeth in secret shall reward thee openly.—Matthew 6:6

■ DAILY BIBLE READINGS

Jan. 3 — A Call to Love Enemies. Matt. 5:43–48
Jan. 4 — Instructions about Alms and Prayer. Matt. 6:1–6
Jan. 5 — The Lord's Prayer. Matt. 6:7–15
Jan. 6 — Ask, Search, Knock: God Will Respond.
Matt. 7:7–11
Jan. 7 — Persevere in Prayer. Luke 11:5–13
Jan. 8 — A Parable on Perseverance in Prayer.
Luke 18:1–8
Jan. 9 — The Pharisee and the Tax Collector.
Luke 18:9–14

Miracles of Compassion

Basic Passage: Matthew 9:18–31, 35–36

Sim's story I will never forget. On his way down a narrow
Kenyan road to witness, he discovered a dear lady, walking
weakly down the road away from the hospital. Through the
caring translators, he quietly inquired why she was turning
away from the hospital. The doctor gave me a prescription
that would heal me, but it costs eight dollars. I could never
find eight dollars, so I cannot get the prescription. One of
the men hurried away to find our van, returned to take the
woman to the pharmacy, paid for the prescription, and gave
life to a woman who saw her life as worth less than eight
dollars. Jesus continues to send His disciples to people with
lives torn apart so He can put them back together.

■ THE BIBLE LESSON

Matthew 9

*18 While he spake these things unto them, behold, there
came a certain ruler, and worshiped him, saying, My daughter is even now dead: but come and lay thy hand upon her,
and she shall live.*

*19 And Jesus arose, and followed him, and so did his dis-
ciples.*

*20 And, behold, a woman, which was diseased with an
issue of blood twelve years, came behind him, and touched
the hem of his garment:*

*21 For she said within herself, If I may but touch his gar-
ment, I shall be whole.*

*22 But Jesus turned him about, and when he saw her, he
said, Daughter, be of good comfort; thy faith hath made thee
whole. And the woman was made whole from that hour.*

*23 And when Jesus came into the ruler's house, and saw
the minstrels and the people making a noise,*

24 He said unto them, Give place: for the maid is not dead, but sleepeth. And they laughed him to scorn.

25 But when the people were put forth, he went in, and took her by the hand, and the maid arose.

26 And the fame hereof went abroad into all that land.

27 And when Jesus departed thence, two blind men followed him, crying, and saying, Thou son of David, have mercy on us.

28 And when he was come into the house, the blind men came to him: and Jesus saith unto them, Believe ye that I am able to do this? They said unto him, Yea, Lord.

29 Then touched he their eyes, saying, According to your faith be it unto you.

30 And their eyes were opened; and Jesus straitly charged them, saying, See that no man know it.

31 But they, when they were departed, spread abroad his fame in all that country.

35 And Jesus went about all the cities and villages, teaching in their synagogues, and preaching the gospel of the kingdom, and healing every sickness and every disease among the people.

36 But when he saw the multitudes, he was moved with compassion on them, because they fainted, and were scattered abroad, as sheep having no shepherd.

THE LESSON EXPLAINED

Faith Seeks Healing (9:18–22)

Illness touches every life. A Jewish religious leader, chief official in a synagogue, sees his daughter aching, weakening, dying. He breaks free from the hatred and opposition his fellow religious leaders feel toward Jesus. Time of need becomes time for faith. He runs to Jesus for help. Seeing the need and the faith, Jesus goes immediately to help.

Interruption! A poor woman, financial and emotional resources dried up after twelve years of fighting illness, wants help, too. Dashing to the dead, Jesus is interrupted by the touch of the sick. Jesus senses healing power used and healing faith exercised. He turns to affirm the fearful woman's act. Faith that seeks Jesus finds Him, often in healing power, always in forgiving salvation.

Faith Finds Fame (9:22–26)

Faith was not the normal response Jesus faces. Scorn more often greeted Him, even from those mourning for the dead. He dismissed their efforts, saying the child was only asleep. They tried to hoot Him out of town. Instead, the synagogue ruler made room for Jesus and dismissed the mourners. The hand of Jesus brought healing to the dead. Scorn turned to surprise, surprise to sensation. Every lip spread the news. Jesus raised the dead child! Who can He be?

Faith Proclaims God's Love (9:27–31)

Fame brought further faith. Blind men wanted to see. Jesus sought more than request for help. He wanted faith in Him. They passed the faith test. Eyes opened. Objects became clear. They could see. Faith had produced enough fame and enough false rumors about His mission. Jesus tried to hush the formerly blind men from testifying. He needed no people trying to use His power for their purposes. Such love, such power, such amazing results could not be hushed. People told what Jesus did.

Faith Feels Empathy and Compassion (9:35,36)

Fame could not limit Jesus. People openly wondering if He were the Messiah, people waiting for Him to show His power as the new Son of David and overthrow Rome to reestablish Jerusalem . . . such people tagged along wherever He went. Still, He extended His ministry—teaching the kingdom, preaching the gospel, healing the sick. But all He could not reach. Multitudes with needs abounded. He was only one person, limited as to the places and people He could reach. With compassion and love for all, He understood their condition. Helpless sheep need a shepherd to guide them to water and pasture. Was He the only One with compassion? Did no one else recognize their need? Oh, where were other laborers who could be their guides and lead them to trust the Good Shepherd?

■ TRUTHS TO LIVE BY

Jesus can make you whole. Pharisees thought they were whole because they were religious. Jesus seeks people who know their needs and see that He alone can meet them. No matter how broken you feel and no matter what social class claims you, Jesus wants to make you whole.

Faith is God's requirement for wholeness. Becoming whole is not a psychological trick. It is not the result of so many hours of therapy, no matter how much therapy may help. Becoming whole is letting God pour Himself into you, so that you become attuned to Him and let Him remake you into the image of Christ. Christ acts when you trust Him to act.

Witnessing is the result of wholeness. Wholeness is more than physical healing or psychological renewal. Wholeness gives new purpose and direction to life. A major purpose for one's life is inviting the broken to become whole. Overjoyed by wholeness, you point others to the Holy One who made you whole.

■ A VERSE TO REMEMBER

But when he saw the multitudes, he was moved with compassion on them, because they fainted, and were scattered abroad, as sheep having no shepherd.—Matthew 9:36

■ DAILY BIBLE READINGS

Jan. 10 — Jesus Continues His Healing Work. Matt. 8:1–13
Jan. 11 — Jesus Heals the Gadarene Demoniacs.
         Matt. 8:28–9:1
Jan. 12 — Jesus Heals a Paralytic. Matt. 9:2–8
Jan. 13 — Jesus Gives Life and Healing. Matt. 9:18–26
Jan. 14 — Jesus Heals the Blind and Mute. Matt. 9:27–38
Jan. 15 — Jesus Heals a Man's Withered Hand. Matt. 12:9–14
Jan. 16 — The Faith of a Canaanite Woman. Matt. 15:21–31

Opposition to Jesus

Basic Passage: Matthew 12:22–32, 38–40

Dilemma of all dilemmas! First day in Kenya. God has led over forty people to faith in Him as He has led me from one thatched roof to another. We return to the village center for our worship service. I want to check with the pastor and translators to make sure I know the program. A woman tugs at my sleeve. Come, she says. What to do? I look to my Kenya brothers. Come, they say. So we go with her, into the small dark room where she lives. Pray for me, she says. I have been sick for many years. No one can heal. Pray God to heal me. Many times I had prayed for the sick in our hospitals, expecting God to use medical services and His power to heal. Here, faith was tested. Did I truly believe God alone could heal?

We prayed together in fervent consent. God, heal this lady. The next day, the lady came running up to us again as we started the worship service. Thank God, thank God. I am healed! Certainly, neither my faith nor my prayer power brought healing. God wanted to show His power where no one could doubt it was His power.

■ THE BIBLE LESSON

Matthew 12

22 Then was brought unto him one possessed with a devil, blind, and dumb: and he healed him, insomuch that the blind and dumb both spake and saw.

23 And all the people were amazed, and said, Is not this the son of David?

24 But when the Pharisees heard it, they said, This fellow doth not cast out devils, but by Beelzebub the prince of the devils.

25 *And Jesus knew their thoughts, and said unto them, Every kingdom divided against itself is brought to desolation; and every city or house divided against itself shall not stand:*

26 *And if Satan cast out Satan, he is divided against himself; how shall then his kingdom stand?*

27 *And if I by Beelzebub cast out devils, by whom do your children cast them out? therefore they shall be your judges.*

28 *But if I cast out devils by the Spirit of God, then the kingdom of God is come unto you.*

29 *Or else how can one enter into a strong man's house, and spoil his goods, except he first bind the strong man? and then he will spoil his house.*

30 *He that is not with me is against me; and he that gathereth not with me scattereth abroad.*

31 *Wherefore I say unto you, All manner of sin and blasphemy shall be forgiven unto men: but the blasphemy against the Holy Ghost shall not be forgiven unto men.*

32 *And whosoever speaketh a word against the Son of man, it shall be forgiven him: but whosoever speaketh against the Holy Ghost, it shall not be forgiven him, neither in this world, neither in the world to come.*

38 *Then certain of the scribes and of the Pharisees answered, saying, Master, we would see a sign from thee.*

39 *But he answered and said unto them, An evil and adulterous generation seeketh after a sign; and there shall no sign be given to it, but the sign of the prophet Jonas:*

40 *For as Jonas was three days and three nights in the whale's belly; so shall the Son of man be three days and three nights in the heart of the earth.*

■ THE LESSON EXPLAINED

Who Can This Be? (12:22–24)

What causes diseases? Germs, viruses, malnutrition. We have all the answers. Well, not quite all. The Bible witnesses to a cause we like to ignore. Satan can cause illness. He can inhabit a person's life and create his special kind of misery. A friend brought such a person to Jesus. Jesus restored sight and sound. Of course, the people responded in amazement. Only one person on earth could accomplish this—Messiah, the anointed One, Son of David, deliverer from Rome.

Minority opinion as usual from the Pharisees. They had religious insight. They could tell what was happening. He follows Beelzebub, the lord of the flies, the chief of all demons. At least that is the way Jews treated Beelzebub. Long before, the Canaanites had probably called this one Baal Zebul, the lord of the heavens or of the heavenly temple. Pharisees and Jesus agreed on this point. Beelzebub was the demon above all demons. Pharisees thought Jesus was the chief agent of the chief demon.

Satan or the Spirit? (12:25–29)

Foolishness! You did not think this one through, Jesus retorted. Civil war splits any kingdom. You cannot fight yourself and win. Satan cannot cast out Satan and come home victorious.

Another perspective. Disciples of the Pharisees, other accredited Jews, also cast out demons. Did the Pharisees mean these also cast them out by the power of Beelzebub? Say that, and you have created civil war in your own camp. Those of your own ilk who cast out demons will condemn you. If they can cast them out by the power of God, so can I. If I cast them out by the Spirit of God as your own evidence seems to indicate, then God is doing His work among you through Me. That means My work shows the presence of His kingdom. See what I am doing. I am entering Satan's domain, binding Satan so he is powerless and destroying all that Satan controls. Is not that the kingdom of God among you?

For Me or Against Me? (12:30–32)

Decision time. For Me? Or not? Do not try to hang on the fence. You must choose. Me or not Me! Eternal destiny hangs in the balance. If you are saying My kingdom-of-God work is really kingdom-of-Satan work, then you are denying the power and work of the Spirit of God. Such blasphemy is the only sin God cannot and will not forgive. It does not matter that you are defaming and scorning Me. That can be forgiven. But to see the work of the Holy Spirit and deny it—that is to deny the power of God. That deserves and receives eternal damnation. Choice is yours. Is the Spirit working through me to establish God's kingdom? Your choice: heaven or hell!

What Sign Gives Proof? (12:38–40)

Jesus, we are not quite satisfied yet. Show us one more all-convincing sign. Do one miracle we can all know is from God alone. Not possible. One more sign you will get, but not what you want. You will get the sign of Jonah. Jonah stayed in the fish's belly three days and then came out. I will stay in the grave three days and come out. That is the only sign you will get. Enough? Me? Or not Me?

■ TRUTHS TO LIVE BY

Opponents doubt Christ's person. Christ's power does not convince the doubter. You have to believe who He is to understand what He does.

Opponents miss God's kingdom. Christ at work is the kingdom at work. If you do not recognize it now, you cannot be part of it then. Opposing Christ now robs you of all opportunity for heaven. You have enough signs to point you to faith in Christ. Don't expect more. The Resurrection is proof positive.

Opponents forsake God's forgiveness. Christ came seeking repentance so He could offer forgiveness. If you cannot see you need to repent, you will never find forgiveness.

▪ A VERSE TO REMEMBER

He that is not with me is against me; and he that gathereth not with me scattereth abroad.—Matthew 12:30

▪ DAILY BIBLE READINGS

Laborers in the Vineyard

Basic Passage: Matthew 20:1–16

Never forget my first paycheck. Went to work in the store where Dad worked. Folded boxes for the baker to put cakes in. Got twenty-five cents an hour. Worked eight hours that first Saturday. Got a check for two dollars. I had never done the math. Just glad to have a job and know I was going to have a lot of money. Then saw the two dollars. Shocked me out of a dream world into reality. It takes a lot of work to make a lot of money. But I got what I agreed to. Jesus had to teach His audience some basic business math, much like Dad taught me.

■ THE BIBLE LESSON

Matthew 20

1 For the kingdom of heaven is like unto a man that is an householder, which went out early in the morning to hire laborers into his vineyard.

2 And when he had agreed with the laborers for a penny a day, he sent them into his vineyard.

3 And he went out about the third hour, and saw others standing idle in the marketplace,

4 And said unto them; Go ye also into the vineyard, and whatsoever is right I will give you. And they went their way.

5 Again he went out about the sixth and ninth hour, and did likewise.

6 And about the eleventh hour he went out, and found others standing idle, and saith unto them, Why stand ye here all the day idle?

7 They say unto him, Because no man hath hired us. He saith unto them, Go ye also into the vineyard; and whatsoever is right, that shall ye receive.

8 So when even was come, the lord of the vineyard saith unto his steward, Call the labourers, and give them their hire, beginning from the last unto the first.

9 And when they came that were hired about the eleventh hour, they received every man a penny.

10 But when the first came, they supposed that they should have received more; and they likewise received every man a penny.

11 And when they had received it, they murmured against the goodman of the house,

12 Saying, These last have wrought but one hour, and thou hast made them equal unto us, which have borne the burden and heat of the day.

13 But he answered one of them, and said, Friend, I do thee no wrong: didst not thou agree with me for a penny?

14 Take that thine is, and go thy way: I will give unto this last, even as unto thee.

15 Is it not lawful for me to do what I will with mine own? Is thine eye evil, because I am good?

16 So the last shall be first, and the first last: for many be called, but few chosen.

THE LESSON EXPLAINED

Knowing the Contract (20:1–2)

Jesus taught His disciples repeatedly in parables, brief stories from daily life that illustrated how God worked on a much grander scale than the small parameters of the parable context. This parable hinges around labor problems. A man in charge of harvesting a crop sought people to harvest it and made a fair deal with them, giving them the denarius or small coin that a person expected to receive for a day's work.

Trusting the Boss (20:3–7)

Harvests can never be collected soon enough. Bad weather always threatens to ruin the harvest, as do hungry animals. The more workers the better. So the labor boss goes to the market to find more workers, again and again. No labor contract with these, just a promise to be fair. The workers trust the boss and go to work.

Grumbling at Grace (20:8–15)

Pay time. Person had to get his wages to feed his family that day. Last shall be first in the pay line. Each came. Each got a denarius even though each had worked only a limited number of hours. What a wonderful boss to give more than I deserve. I can feed my family today even without working a full day. Then the contracted workers came. They wanted grace more abundant. Two denarii perhaps. After all, they had outworked all the rest. But no! They got what the contract called for: one denarius. Unfair! Unfair! He cheated us!

What's unfair? You got the going wage. You got what you agreed to. Are you mad because I am gracious to the others so they can feed their families? It's my money. I can do with it as I wish. Do you become greedy and evil because I show grace to other people?

Called, Not Chosen (20:16)

Kingdom ways can be confusing to earthlings. We value people in different ways than God does. The ones we think are head of the line, He sends to the foot. The ones we ignore as useless, He calls to the head of the class. Willing to let Him make the decisions? You are among His chosen. Want things operated according to standards you set and values you define? Go to the foot of the line. All depends on God's grace. Trust Him, and enjoy the rewards He gives. Don't try to go back to legalism. You will never fulfill the contract and earn more than God offers.

■ TRUTHS TO LIVE BY

God rewards more than you deserve. You can focus on how God treats other people. Or you can focus on how God treats you. You will never understand God's grace. It is beyond human understanding. You can certainly enjoy that grace, if you do not try to reduce it to a contract He has with you.

God rewards those who trust Him. God wants a free relationship with you, one where you obey Him because you trust Him to be more than fair. He does not want you to negotiate every detail and try to hold Him to the negotiated minutiae. Then He has to hold you to the contract, too. With God you will get more than you deserve.

God's grace is not on the bargaining table. God rewards on His terms, not ours. Kingdom work is not like earthly labor, where you work for a paycheck. With God, you work because He showed His love before you ever went to work.

■ A VERSE TO REMEMBER

So the last shall be first, and the first last: for many be called, but few chosen.—Matthew 20:16.

■ DAILY BIBLE READINGS

Jan. 24 — The Rich Young Man and Jesus.
　　　　　Matt. 19:16–22
Jan. 25 — All Things Are Possible for God. Matt. 19:23–30
Jan. 26 — Hiring of Laborers for the Vineyard. Matt. 20:1–7
Jan. 27 — God's Grace Illustrated in a Parable. Matt. 20:8–16
Jan. 28 — Jesus' Death and Resurrection Foretold.
　　　　　Matt. 20:17–23
Jan. 29 — Jesus Teaches about Servanthood.
　　　　　Matt. 20:24–28
Jan. 30 — Jesus Demonstrates Servanthood.
　　　　　John 13:1–15

Coming to Jerusalem

Basic Passage: Matthew 21:1–13

Church bulletins reveal much about the way we do church. They show how many people attended last week, how much money was given, how much below budget currents gifts are, how many meetings people should attend. Is this the way Jesus wants to do church? Is this the way to respond to the King as He comes to us?

■ THE BIBLE LESSON

Matthew 21

1 And when they drew nigh unto Jerusalem, and were come to Bethphage, unto the mount of Olives, then sent Jesus two disciples,

2 Saying unto them, Go into the village over against you, and straightway ye shall find an ass tied, and a colt with her: loose them, and bring them unto me.

3 And if any man say aught unto you, ye shall say, The Lord hath need of them; and straightway he will send them.

4 All this was done, that it might be fulfilled which was spoken by the prophet, saying,

5 Tell ye the daughter of Sion, Behold, thy King cometh unto thee, meek, and sitting upon an ass, and a colt the foal of an ass.

6 And the disciples went, and did as Jesus commanded them,

7 And brought the ass, and the colt, and put on them their clothes, and they set him thereon.

8 And a very great multitude spread their garments in the way; others cut down branches from the trees, and strawed them in the way.

9 And the multitudes that went before, and that followed, cried, saying, Hosanna to the son of David: Blessed is he that cometh in the name of the Lord; Hosanna in the highest.

10 And when he was come into Jerusalem, all the city was moved, saying, Who is this?

11 And the multitude said, This is Jesus the prophet of Nazareth of Galilee.

12 And Jesus went into the temple of God, and cast out all them that sold and bought in the temple, and overthrew the tables of the moneychangers, and the seats of them that sold doves,

13 And said unto them, It is written, My house shall be called the house of prayer; but ye have made it a den of thieves.

THE LESSON EXPLAINED

The Lord's Need (21:1-6)

Passion week. Jesus enters Jerusalem, knowing opposition, persecution, and crucifixion await. Jesus walks over the Mount of Olives, east of Jerusalem. Taking a break, He sends two disciples on a special mission. Find a donkey and its colt. Bring them to me. If someone objects, just say, the Lord needs them. You will find no more objections. Come to me. Thus, Jesus made sure messianic Scripture in Zechariah 9:9 and Isaiah 62:11 was fulfilled, but in His own way, with a donkey and a colt, not with war chargers ready for battle.

The Lord's Blessing (27:7-11)

Obedient disciples brought the animals to Jesus, used their clothes for a saddle to make the ride more comfortable, and waited to see what would happen. The commotion drew crowds, especially since it involved this notorious teacher named Jesus. Crowds rejoiced in His coming. They treated Him like a king, throwing their clothes as a "red carpet" for Him to ride on. They threw down palm branches reserved for a victorious king. They sang praises to Him as Messiah, Son of David, new king of Jerusalem. No one could ignore His entry. Neither could they understand it. Who was this? What was going on? The celebrating crowd knew: this was the prophet from Nazareth in Galilee come to Jerusalem to claim His crown.

The Lord's House (21:12,13)

Jesus did not go to the palace to claim a crown. He went to God's house to clean a commercial house. Yes, worship had created a new market niche: animals and incense and coins for sacrifice. Offering "services" and making money overshadowed offering sacrifices and making prayers. A refuge from the world had become a replica of the world. A home for forgiveness became an opportunity for cutthroat business and robbery. Jesus had to clean it up.

■ TRUTHS TO LIVE BY

Christ the King fulfills Scripture. Jesus knew He was Israel's promised Messiah. He consciously acted out Scripture to show He was, but He did it in ways that changed hopes Israel had created of political power to hopes God had for saving spiritual purposes.

Christ the King deserves praise. Christ is Messiah, God in human flesh. Praise and worship are man's only adequate and suitable responses.

Christ the King sees prayer, not profit. Too often the church measures itself by the world's standards. Christ throws all such standards in the trash. He measures His church by how it prays and how it reveals God's love and forgiveness.

■ A VERSE TO REMEMBER

Tell ye the daughter of Sion, Behold, thy King cometh unto thee, meek, and sitting upon an ass, and a colt the foal of an ass.—Matthew 21:5

■ **DAILY BIBLE READINGS**

Jan. 31 — Jesus Sets His Face Toward Jerusalem.
Luke 9:51–56
Feb. 1 — Jesus Enters Jerusalem Amid Hosannas.
Matt. 21:1–11
Feb. 2 — Jesus Cleanses the Temple. Matt. 21:12–17
Feb. 3 — Chief Priests and Elders Resist Jesus.
Matt. 21:23–27
Feb. 4 — Parable of the Wicked Tenants. Matt. 21:33–46
Feb. 5 — A Question about the Resurrection.
Matt. 22:23–33
Feb. 6 — The Greatest Commandment of All.
Matt. 22:34–46

Watching for Christ's Return

Basic Passage: Matthew 24:45–25:13

Teaching is my passion. I love to take God's Word into a group of people who want to hear God speak. I love to ask questions and get the group involved in searching for what God has to say to them. What an exhilaration to come home knowing God has used me to help people see something in His Word they had never seen before or to find direction in the specific circumstances of their lives that they had prayed desperately for. Sometimes that just does not happen. I come home knowing nothing happened today. We read the Word and asked the questions and directed the discussion, but somehow answers did not come and directions did not flow.

What makes the difference? Most often, the difference is in the preparation I have made. Am I teaching out of an overflow of experience with God in prayer? Am I teaching out of a time of extended study of God's Word? Or am I trying to teach out of past experiences and past study? Am I depending on what I know and what I have accomplished? Or am I prepared because I have been with God? One day each of us gets to answer this question one last time: Are you prepared?

■ THE BIBLE LESSON

Matthew 24

45 Who then is a faithful and wise servant, whom his lord hath made ruler over his household, to give them meat in due season?

46 Blessed is that servant, whom his lord when he cometh shall find so doing.

47 Verily I say unto you, That he shall make him ruler over all his goods.

48 But and if that evil servant shall say in his heart, My lord delayeth his coming;

49 And shall begin to smite his fellow servants, and to eat and drink with the drunken;

50 *The lord of that servant shall come in a day when he looketh not for him, and in an hour that he is not aware of,*

51 *And shall cut him asunder, and appoint him his portion with the hypocrites: there shall be weeping and gnashing of teeth.*

· ·

Matthew 25

1 *Then shall the kingdom of heaven be likened unto ten virgins, which took their lamps, and went forth to meet the bridegroom.*

2 *And five of them were wise, and five were foolish.*

3 *They that were foolish took their lamps, and took no oil with them:*

4 *But the wise took oil in their vessels with their lamps.*

5 *While the bridegroom tarried, they all slumbered and slept.*

6 *And at midnight there was a cry made, Behold, the bridegroom cometh; go ye out to meet him.*

7 *Then all those virgins arose, and trimmed their lamps.*

8 *And the foolish said unto the wise, Give us of your oil; for our lamps are gone out.*

9 *But the wise answered, saying, Not so; lest there be not enough for us and you: but go ye rather to them that sell, and buy for yourselves.*

10 *And while they went to buy, the bridegroom came; and they that were ready went in with him to the marriage: and the door was shut.*

11 *Afterward came also the other virgins, saying, Lord, Lord, open to us.*

12 *But he answered and said, Verily I say unto you, I know you not.*

13 *Watch therefore, for ye know neither the day nor the hour wherein the Son of man cometh.*

■ **THE LESSON EXPLAINED**

Faithful Without Supervision (24:45–51)

Job description: Administer the owner's business while he is gone. Make sure all the employees have what they need. Danger: The owner will come back unannounced. Compensation: Promotion beyond imagination or description; second in command to the owner.

How the situation usually works: Administrator becomes self-confident and arrogant. He shows his power over the other employees so they will be sure who is boss. He throws parties and becomes one of the fellows in drunken brawls. He forgets who is boss. Result: Owner returns unexpectedly. Situation clear to the owner. Administrator leaves the party to become party to eternal punishment.

Preparing for the Return (25:1–9)

Eternity is too much to grasp, so Jesus told stories about it. Eternity begins here on earth in life with Him. Here we are enjoying His presence but waiting for His fulness. Two types of people are involved in the waiting. It is like preparing to attend a wedding. First step in the wedding process is to accompany the bridegroom to the bride's house for the wedding. Never know when the bridegroom will decide to come. Finally, sleepy eyes win out. Suddenly, without warning, the groom appears, at midnight of all times. Get up. Trim your lamps, so you can light the groom's way. Oh, no! Oil's all burned out. What now? Oh, you all have extra oil. Share with us. Cannot do. We need all we have. Go, buy more oil for yourself. Should have been prepared!

Missing His Coming (25:10–12)

Off to the oil supply store. Here comes the groom. Can't wait for the others. Must go with Him. All's set for the wedding. Have to go on without the other bridemaids. Ceremony's almost over. Someone's knocking at the door. Sorry, too late. Can't let you in now. I recognize only people who come prepared. No second chance. No preparations after the marriage feast has started.

Call to Watch (25:13)

What does this story have to do with me? It illustrates how Jesus will come back to earth. The day will never appear on your calendar. No warning to be ready except what you already have. No second chance when He comes. If you have not trusted Him in faith and lived as His disciple, you cannot do so when He suddenly appears. That is judgment time, not conversion time. Trust Him to save you now. Then you will be prepared for His coming, whenever it is.

TRUTHS TO LIVE BY

God's servants obey always. You cannot play by your rules today and expect to be ready for judgment by God's rules tomorrow. When Christ returns, He does not offer a second chance to repent and get things right. He has offered the grace of salvation today. Now is the time to accept Him and obey Him. Then you will be ready whenever He returns.

God's servants are prepared for His return. Preparing for Christ means one thing: dedicating your life to Him for today and always. You cannot try to second guess God and decide to get ready for Him just in the nick of time. You cannot outsmart Him. Why would you want to? What He offers here and hereafter is always a better life than you can create for yourself. Trust Him now. He will take care of you now and then.

God's servants trust God's timing. God is all knowing and all loving. He will return and end earth's history at just the right moment. Trust Him to do so.

A VERSE TO REMEMBER

Watch therefore, for ye know neither the day nor the hour wherein the Son of man cometh.—Matthew 25:13

DAILY BIBLE READINGS

Feb. 7 — Signs of the End. Matt. 24:1–8
Feb. 8 — Jesus' Followers Will Be Persecuted. Matt. 24:9–14
Feb. 9 — Beware of False Messiahs. Matt. 24:15–28
Feb. 10 — Coming of the Son of Man. Matt. 24:29–35
Feb. 11 — Be Watchful and Expectant. Matt. 24:36–44
Feb. 12 — Call to Be Faithful Servants. Matt. 24:45–51
Feb. 13 — Parable of the Ten Bridesmaids. Matt. 25:1–13

Death of Jesus

Basic Passage: Matthew 27:38–54

I spent yesterday afternoon with my grief group. Six people who have lost spouses and are trying to find new meaning and new direction for life in the face of death. Two years have passed for most of us since we stared death in the eye. The ones still attending the grief group are finding tears come much less often, hope begins to glimmer on the horizon, and life has purpose and direction again. But some original members of the group have isolated themselves from us and from life. Phone conversations quickly show that despair and darkness continue to fill life. They remind us that one death at the center of history is the key to hope and despair, life and death for all of us.

■ THE BIBLE LESSON

Matthew 27

38 Then were there two thieves crucified with him, one on the right hand, and another on the left.

39 And they that passed by reviled him, wagging their heads,

40 And saying, Thou that destroyest the temple, and buildest it in three days, save thyself. If thou be the Son of God, come down from the cross.

41 Likewise also the chief priests mocking him, with the scribes and elders, said,

42 He saved others; himself he cannot save. If he be the King of Israel, let him now come down from the cross, and we will believe him.

43 He trusted in God; let him deliver him now, if he will have him: for he said, I am the Son of God.

44 The thieves also, which were crucified with him, cast the same in his teeth.

45 Now from the sixth hour there was darkness over all the land unto the ninth hour.

46 And about the ninth hour Jesus cried with a loud voice, saying, Eli, Eli, lama sabachthani? that is to say, My God, my God, why hast thou forsaken me?

47 Some of them that stood there, when they heard that, said, This man calleth for Elias.

48 And straightway one of them ran, and took a spunge, and filled it with vinegar, and put it on a reed, and gave him to drink.

49 The rest said, Let be, let us see whether Elias will come to save him.

50 Jesus, when he had cried again with a loud voice, yielded up the ghost.

51 And, behold, the veil of the temple was rent in twain from the top to the bottom; and the earth did quake, and the rocks rent;

52 And the graves were opened; and many bodies of the saints which slept arose,

53 And came out of the graves after his resurrection, and went into the holy city, and appeared unto many.

54 Now when the centurion, and they that were with him, watching Jesus, saw the earthquake, and those things that were done, they feared greatly, saying, Truly this was the Son of God.

▮ THE LESSON EXPLAINED

Save Yourself, Son of God (27:38–44)

Crowds gather. Disciples flee. Jews want the sign—This is Jesus the King of the Jews—dismantled or at least altered. Two thieves pay for their crimes with their lives, but only their families notice. All eyes focus on the central cross. People passing by spit, scream, and scorn. You said if the temple were destroyed, You would build it back in three days. What power You claimed. Now look. A criminal on a cross. Show Your power. Save Yourself. Son of God!

Yeah, sure. Prove it. Come down from that cross. The insti-
gators of the crucifixion chimed in: Look at Him. Saved others, He did, with His healings and such. Why doesn't He
save Himself, come down from the cross? Then we can
believe. Claimed to have so much faith in God. Where is God
for Him now? How can He be the Son of God on a cross?
Even the dying thieves took up the chorus. What does it
take to prove you are the Son of God?

God-forsaken, Dying Son of God (27:45–50)

Eerie, it is. Noontime and pitch dark. Three hours of
absolute darkness. What can this mean? Listen, what is He
saying? He quotes Psalm 22:1, asking why God has forsaken Him. Did God take this moment to prove all Jesus'
claims to be false? Oh, no! Jesus took on Himself the
burden of all human sin. Such sin could not enter the holy
presence of God. Thus, Jesus, even though He had not
sinned Himself, experienced the deepest despair of humanity, the feeling of separation and isolation from God that
only sin can bring. The crowd mistook His Aramaic prayer
as a desperation call for Elijah to come and rescue Him. Elijah's role had been at the transfiguration (ch. 17), not at the
crucifixion. Someone felt a bit of compassion and tries to
quench His thirst with the cheap vinegar wine that poor
people drank. Meanwhile, Jesus died, bearing our sins.

Religion-changing, Death-defying Son of God (27:51–54)

Jesus' death did not slip by unnoticed. The veil of the
temple separating the holy of holies from public view split
in two. Religion no longer separated the duties of priests
and laity. Through Jesus, all have access directly to God.
Yearly atonement rituals are outdated. Jesus has atoned for
sin once for all. The earth quaked, breaking huge boulders.
Graves opened, allowing the dead to rise momentarily. Such
events are not fabulous tales concocted by a few secret
believers. The general public saw what was happening. So
did the leader of the Roman army unit at the cross with his

troops. For them fear of nature turned to fear of God, as they confessed, "Certainly, this was the Son of God."

■ TRUTHS TO LIVE BY

Jesus died, fulfilling God's ways, not ours. No human think tank would devise a plan of salvation centered on a cross. Human minds would not dream up a God dying for human sin. Humans scorned and sneered. Christ suffered. God provided salvation.

Jesus experienced God's absence for us. Physical pain was not Jesus' worst reality on the cross. Spiritual pain of feeling separated from—out of contact with—the Father was His greatest pain. He did nothing to deserve the physical or the spiritual pain. He suffered that we might live eternally.

Jesus' death proved He was God's Son. Those most closely involved in killing Jesus, the Roman soldiers and their commander, watched all that happened and then bowed their heads in worship and confession. God showed at the cross itself through nature, through the temple veil, and through empty tombs that Jesus is the Son of God.

■ A VERSE TO REMEMBER

Now when the centurion, and they that were with him, watching Jesus, saw the earthquake, and those things that were done, they feared greatly, saying, Truly this was the Son of God.—Matthew 27:54

■ DAILY BIBLE READINGS

Feb. 14 — Jesus Delivered to Pilate; Judas's Suicide. Matt. 27:1–10

Feb. 15 — Jesus Before Pilate. Matt. 27:11–18

Feb. 16 — The Crowd Agitates for Barabbas's Release. Matt. 27:19–23

Feb. 17 — Jesus Is Handed over for Crucifixion. Matt. 27:24–31

Feb. 18 — Jesus Is Crucified. Matt. 27:32–44

Feb. 19 — Jesus Dies. Matt. 27:45–56

Feb. 20 — Jesus Is Buried. Matt. 27:57–61

Resurrection and Commission

Basic Passage: Matthew 28:1–10, 16–20

It's tough to watch the struggle. The brilliant young worker just out of college on his first job. College has shown him the way to computerize and modernize. Company where he now works does it the old-fashioned way, the way that has worked for them for more than a century. He tries sharing a suggestion or two with the boss that would speed up processes, add efficiency, and ultimately affect the bottom line positively. Nothing happens. The young grad with knowledge has met the old system with authority. How long will it take for youth to learn how to cope with authority? Jesus, too, struggled with an authority system. After His resurrection, He could show His disciples where all authority lies.

■ THE BIBLE LESSON

Matthew 28

1 In the end of the sabbath, as it began to dawn toward the first day of the week, came Mary Magdalene and the other Mary to see the sepulchre.

2 And, behold, there was a great earthquake: for the angel of the Lord descended from heaven, and came and rolled back the stone from the door, and sat upon it.

3 His countenance was like lightning, and his raiment white as snow:

4 And for fear of him the keepers did shake, and became as dead men.

5 And the angel answered and said unto the women, Fear not ye: for I know that ye seek Jesus, which was crucified.

6 He is not here: for he is risen, as he said. Come, see the place where the Lord lay.

7 And go quickly, and tell his disciples that he is risen from the dead; and, behold, he goeth before you into Galilee; there shall ye see him: lo, I have told you.

8 And they departed quickly from the sepulchre with fear and great joy; and did run to bring his disciples word.

9 And as they went to tell his disciples, behold, Jesus met them, saying, All hail. And they came and held him by the feet, and worshiped him.

10 Then said Jesus unto them, Be not afraid: go tell my brethren that they go into Galilee, and there shall they see me.

16 Then the eleven disciples went away into Galilee, into a mountain where Jesus had appointed them.

17 And when they saw him, they worshiped him: but some doubted.

18 And Jesus came and spake unto them, saying, All power is given unto me in heaven and in earth.

19 Go ye therefore, and teach all nations, baptizing them in the name of the Father, and of the Son, and of the Holy Ghost:

20 Teaching them to observe all things whatsoever I have commanded you: and, lo, I am with you always, even unto the end of the world. Amen.

THE LESSON EXPLAINED

God in Action (28:1–4)

All was lost. Only one thing left to do. Carry out the duties you owe to the dead. So as the sun came up on the first day of a new week and, unbeknownst to them, on the first day of a new faith, the women dutifully made their way through the streets of Jerusalem to the tomb.

Startled, they stood back. The earth shook. Cracks appeared in the ground. The sky darkened. The tomb was open, the seal of the Roman government (27:66) broken. No stone in front of it. The posted Roman guards frozen in a coma of fear.

No Longer Dead—Now Alive (28:5–8)

A voice spoke. Don't be afraid. You are looking for Jesus, the one the Romans executed on the cross. He is no longer here. He is risen from the dead. Let me show you where His body was. Yes, let me show you the beginning of the Christian faith, the center of faith's uniqueness. We have an empty tomb. It proves God's power and authority—power and authority greater than any government's, even Rome's. Yes, here is what Christ promised, but you were so caught up in the shock and sadness of the trial and crucifixion that you could not hear. God has shown Jesus to be what He claimed to be: Son of God, Son of Man, Messiah, King of the Jews, Savior, Lord. Resurrection is the proof Jesus and the church are right.

Enough talking. Go tell the disciples this good news. He will meet them in Galilee, where you all walked together during these years of ministry. So off they ran, joy and fear and awe fighting for control of their emotions.

Seeing the Risen Christ (28:9,10)

Stop. Don't run off so fast. Let me greet you personally. To the ground. Forehead on His feet. Yes, bow before Him in worship. It is Jesus Himself. The only response to the resurrected Lord is worship and humility. What? He has a mission for us. Just what the angel said: Go get the disciples to go to Galilee and meet Him. Surely we will do whatever the Resurrected One says!

Witnessing to the Authoritative Christ (28:16–20)

Resurrection was not enough to overcome self-interest. Priests and Romans plotted to deny and refute the real story (vv. 11–15). Disciples retreated from Jerusalem to Galilee, obeying the Master's command. He came. They fell down in worship. In the back of the mind doubts lingered. Is resurrection really possible? Are we fooling ourselves and making fools of ourselves? Then Jesus spoke: God has given Me all power over things in heaven and things in earth. That is what resurrection means. I am the authority in this world and the one to come. Now show that you acknowledge that authority. Go into all the world and share the good news. Tell people they have no reason to fear earthly authorities. They have power for a moment. I have it for eternity. So, go. Start My church. Baptize those who believe in Me in My name, the Father's name, and the Spirit's name. Learn what it means that God has appeared to you and thus exists as three separate persons in one Godhead. Just as you accept My authority, teach people everywhere to do so. You know My teachings. Get everyone to follow them. Don't be afraid. You will always have My presence with you.

■ TRUTHS TO LIVE BY

The Crucified One lives. This central confession separates our faith from all other religions. Christ conquered death. We will, too, through Him. His resurrection guarantees our hope and gives authority to our teaching about Him.

The Risen One deserves our worship. Resurrection shows Jesus is God, part of the eternal Trinity. We have only one response to God—fall on our knees in humble adoration and worship. Give Him the glory! Hallelujah!

The Worshiped One tells us to testify. The Resurrected One is present with you. He has a command for you. If you truly believe He is the divine Son raised from death, then tell everyone about Him and lead them to faith and obedience.

■ A VERSE TO REMEMBER

Go ye therefore, and teach all nations, baptizing them in the name of the Father, and of the Son, and of the Holy Ghost: Teaching them to observe all things whatsoever I have commanded you: and, lo, I am with you alway, even unto the end of the world. Amen.—Matthew 28:19, 20

■ DAILY BIBLE READINGS

Helping a Church Confront Crisis

Basic Passage: 1 Corinthians 1:2–17

We turn from Gospel to letter, from story to teaching, from Galilee to Greece, from Jerusalem to Corinth, from confused, proud, argumentative disciples to a divided, power-hungry, argumentative church. During his second missionary journey, Paul with Aquilla and Priscilla, Silas and Timothy began the church there about A.D. 51 (see Acts 18). After eighteen months in Corinth, Paul continued his missionary journey, but he never forgot the church.

He wrote them a letter that was not preserved (1 Cor. 5:9) and received at least one in return (7:1). He maintained contact with their representatives (1:11; 16:17) and sent his to them (4:8–17). He knew of church divisions, fractured loyalties, and moral problems. After writing 1 Corinthians from Ephesus about A.D. 54 to 56, he endured a painful visit with them himself (2 Cor. 2:1). He wrote another letter, also lost, calling for repentance (2 Cor. 2:4–11) and learned from Titus that the Corinthians eagerly awaited a visit from him (2 Cor. 7:5–16). Paul wrote 2 Corinthians from Macedonia about A.D. 56 or 57 and eventually had a third visit (2 Cor. 12:14; 13:1, 2; Acts 20:2).

■ THE BIBLE LESSON:

1 Corinthians 1

2 Unto the church of God which is at Corinth, to them that are sanctified in Christ Jesus, called to be saints, with all that in every place call upon the name of Jesus Christ our Lord, both theirs and ours:

3 Grace be unto you, and peace, from God our Father, and from the Lord Jesus Christ.

4 I thank my God always on your behalf, for the grace of God which is given you by Jesus Christ;

5 That in every thing ye are enriched by him, in all utterance, and in all knowledge;

6 Even as the testimony of Christ was confirmed in you:

7 So that ye come behind in no gift; waiting for the coming of our Lord Jesus Christ:

8 Who shall also confirm you unto the end, that ye may be blameless in the day of our Lord Jesus Christ.

9 God is faithful, by whom ye were called unto the fellowship of his Son Jesus Christ our Lord.

10 Now I beseech you, brethren, by the name of our Lord Jesus Christ, that ye all speak the same thing, and that there be no divisions among you; but that ye be perfectly joined together in the same mind and in the same judgment.

11 For it hath been declared unto me of you, my brethren, by them which are of the house of Chloe, that there are contentions among you.

12 Now this I say, that every one of you saith, I am of Paul; and I of Apollos; and I of Cephas; and I of Christ.

13 Is Christ divided? Was Paul crucified for you? Or were ye baptized in the name of Paul?

14 I thank God that I baptized none of you, but Crispus and Gaius;

15 Lest any should say that I had baptized in mine own name.

16 And I baptized also the household of Stephanas: besides, I know not whether I baptized any other.

17 For Christ sent me not to baptize, but to preach the gospel: not with wisdom of words, lest the cross of Christ should be made of none effect.

■ THE LESSON EXPLAINED

Church of Christ's Grace (1:2-9)

Paul used the normal form that people writing in Greek in his day used to write letters. He introduced himself, those with him as he wrote, and the persons or church to whom he wrote, gave greetings, and offered thanks (vv. 1-9). Then he turned to the body of the letter with his true purpose. For Corinth, split with leadership loyalties, he identified himself strongly as one sent by God, an apostle with authority from Jesus Christ. He reminded them what it means to be a church of Jesus Christ. Being in Jesus means being holy, set apart to live a pure life according to the authoritative teaching of Jesus and the apostles. Only such people can be called "saints" or holy ones. The church is not limited to one place. It includes all those everywhere who honor Jesus as Lord.

Paul gives greetings to the church, joining the traditional Greek *charis*, or grace, with the Hebrew *shalom* or wholeness and peace. He wants the church to live in a sense of having received God's love without deserving it and having the daily experience of wholeness and assurance in life. Such can come only from God the Father and Son.

Paul gave thanks that the church had received Christ's grace, ensuring them salvation and had received gifts of speaking and knowledge from Him, gifts Paul would later discuss in detail (chs. 12-15). Thus the church appeared to be ready for Christ to return, but Paul would show them some things that needed changing before Christ came back. So Paul could affirm God's faithfulness in calling them to the fellowship with Christ. Now he could ask about their faithfulness in maintaining that fellowship with Christ and with one another.

Church Called to Christ's Unity (1:10-16)

God's grace and gifts do not a church make. The church must utilize those in a unified voice and mission representing Christ in the world. Corinth did not meet that standard. Paul called them to do so. How did the absent Paul know this? He had sources and feared not to name them—Chloe and her family members and servants. Corinth knew Chloe, her relationship to Paul, and her knowledge of the affairs at Corinth. We know nothing of Chloe except her mention here.

The problem at Corinth: divided loyalties. Some looked to Paul for leadership; others to the orator Apollos (Acts 18:24–19:1; 1 Cor. 3:4–6; 15:12; Titus 3:13); others to Peter, Christ's chief apostle of Pentecost (Matt. 16; Acts 1–5; 9:32–12:24); and the more pious members looked only to Christ Himself for leadership. Paul called for unity, defusing the problem by saying he did not deserve consideration as leader, for he did not baptize them, and those few he baptized were baptized into the name of Jesus, not the name of Paul. People fighting over human leaders do not know the fellowship of Jesus (v. 9).

Church Sent to Preach (1:17)

Fellowship with Jesus means preaching Jesus, not defending one human leader against another. Preaching means telling people the foolishness of the cross, not relying on oratorical skills as could Apollos. Fellowship meant the fellowship of taking the cross and walking with Jesus to death, not hearing this and uttering Satanic words of rebuke and denial as Peter had done (Mark 8). So Paul called the church to unity of fellowship, which means unity of preaching.

■ TRUTHS TO LIVE BY

The church exists only through God's grace. No person or church can proudly claim responsibility for starting and maintaining a church. No human leader can demand authority over other people. Christ gave His life, and God in love forgave sinful, undeserving people. That's how the church is founded and that's how it exists today and forever.

The church is called to unity, not divided loyalty. God uses human leaders for His people's good, but He does not want leaders to bring splits and disruptions in His church. Leaders must hide themselves behind the cross and preach Christ crucified. Loyalty belongs to Jesus and no one else.

The church is sent to preach, not compete. Church is not an athletic event where some go home winners and others losers. Church is a unified fellowship supporting one another and testifying by lifestyle and by word of the grace and love of God in Christ. Seek no praise nor power for self. Seek Christ and Him crucified and glorified.

■ A VERSE TO REMEMBER

Now I beseech you, brethren, by the name of our Lord Jesus Christ, that ye all speak the same thing, and that there be no divisions among you; but that ye be perfectly joined together in the same mind and in the same judgment.
—1 Corinthians 1:10

■ DAILY BIBLE READINGS

Feb. 28 — Paul Greets the Corinthian Christians.
1 Cor. 1:1–9

Feb. 29 — Divisions Among Corinthian Christians.
1 Cor. 1:10–17

Mar. 1 — God's Power and Wisdom in Christ.
1 Cor. 1:18–25

Mar. 2 — Christ Jesus, Source of Our Life.
1 Cor. 1:26–31

Mar. 3 — Paul Encourages Timothy. 2 Tim. 1:3–14

Mar. 4 — Serve Jesus Christ Faithfully. 2 Tim. 2:1–13

Mar. 5 — The Ways of God's Servant. 2 Tim. 2:14–26

The Holy Spirit as Teacher

Basic Passage: 1 Corinthians 2:1, 2, 4–13, 15, 16

From earliest childhood throughout life, hurt and bewilderment have followed me as I watched God's church fight among themselves. My earliest memory is of wonderful friends leaving my home church to start a mission. I knew the reason. They did not think the pastor was a strong enough leader. From Texas to Kentucky to Georgia to Germany to Switzerland and back to Tennessee, I have watched churches repeat this fatal practice. We look too much like Corinth and not enough like Jesus. Why?

■ THE BIBLE LESSON

1 Corinthians 2

1 And I, brethren, when I came to you, came not with excellency of speech or of wisdom, declaring unto you the testimony of God.

2 For I determined not to know anything among you, save Jesus Christ, and him crucified.

4 And my speech and my preaching was not with enticing words of man's wisdom, but in demonstration of the Spirit and of power:

5 That your faith should not stand in the wisdom of men, but in the power of God.

6 Howbeit we speak wisdom among them that are perfect: yet not the wisdom of this world, nor of the princes of this world, that come to nought:

7 But we speak the wisdom of God in a mystery, even the hidden wisdom, which God ordained before the world unto our glory:

8 Which none of the princes of this world knew: for had they known it, they would not have crucified the Lord of glory.

9 But as it is written, Eye hath not seen, nor ear heard, neither have entered into the heart of man, the things which God hath prepared for them that love him.

10 But God hath revealed them unto us by his Spirit: for the Spirit searcheth all things, yea, the deep things of God.

11 For what man knoweth the things of a man, save the spirit of man which is in him? even so the things of God knoweth no man, but the Spirit of God.

12 Now we have received, not the spirit of the world, but the spirit which is of God; that we might know the things that are freely given to us of God.

13 Which things also we speak, not in the words which man's wisdom teacheth, but which the Holy Ghost teacheth; comparing spiritual things with spiritual.

15 But he that is spiritual judgeth all things, yet he himself is judged of no man.

16 For who hath known the mind of the Lord, that he may instruct him? But we have the mind of Christ.

▇ THE LESSON EXPLAINED

Christ Alone (2:1, 2)

Personal testimony often opens the door for audiences to listen when any other approach would meet deaf ears. Paul opened himself to the people with broken heart. They knew his preaching style. Certainly it was not marked with human wisdom or style. Only the subject mattered: telling people about God. Preaching does not center on personal abilities or personal experiences. Preaching goes right to the cross and preaches how Jesus died for you. Don't spend time arguing about human style or leadership. Tell people about Jesus, and thank Jesus for what He did for you.

God's Wisdom Alone (2:4–8)

What does preaching show off? Too many people want it to demonstrate the latest techniques of eloquence or the latest findings of scholarship and archaeology. Gospel preaching shows something else. Focus fades from the preacher. Spotlight comes up on the Spirit and His power to persuade. Preaching points beyond the preacher to the One preached. Why? Because faith in the preacher leads only to disappointment and weakness. Faith must be in God and His power.

Surely, preaching involves wisdom. No one wants to hear something that makes no sense and leads to no purpose. Preaching has its own kind of wisdom, a wisdom that leads you away from any person and leads you to God. This wisdom shows you no human achievement. It concentrates on God's achievement: God has fulfilled His purposes in Jesus Christ. Worldly study and worldly wisdom would never know this. Worldly wisdom crucifies Christ. God's wisdom proclaims Christ. Only a person to whom God has revealed His secrets, His mysteries, will know it. That person must preach God's wisdom, not human wisdom.

God's Spirit Alone (7:9–13)

How can a mere human know such wisdom? Read Scripture. It shows you. Look at Isaiah 64:4. Humans cannot find wisdom. God prepares it and gives it to those He loves. How does God do it? He sends His Spirit into our hearts to show us the truth. He is the only One able to send the Spirit and to show the mysteries of God. We must choose: control by human spirit or by God's Spirit in our lives. God's Spirit shows us how to use God's gifts. Thus, our preaching is through God's Spirit intended for God's people who have let God's Spirit make them spiritual rather than worldly people.

Christ's Mind Alone (2:15,16)

It is up to you. Let God's Spirit direct your life, then you are able to judge what is true and what is not, not by human criteria but by the Spirit living in you. You need not fear. The world cannot stand in judgment over you if the Spirit controls you. The world may call you foolish, but that is unimportant to the spiritual person. But what does that say when you choose Apollos or Peter or Paul? It means you are using worldly standards to judge a leader. You are splitting the church. You are obviously not letting the Spirit guide you. You are not spiritual. If you want fellowship with Jesus, you must let Jesus' mind guide you, not worldly wisdom.

■ TRUTHS TO LIVE BY

Successful preaching concentrates on Christ's crucifixion. Too much preaching concentrates on making the preacher look good rather than making Christ look good. The star of the show in Christian worship and Christian preaching is Christ, not the preacher of the moment. Hide behind the cross and show the meaning of the cross. That is preaching.

Successful preaching depends on the Spirit's wisdom and power. Too often preaching shows off the latest book read or the latest fault of the government, school, or church. Education, reading, knowledge of current events may give depth and content to preaching, but it goes for naught if the Spirit is not guiding and giving power to preaching. Preach in the Spirit, not in the library.

Successful preaching reflects the mind of Christ. Too often congregations want the opinion of the preacher. The preacher has no opinion in the pulpit. The preacher reflects only what Christ has told Him through the Spirit. Listen to what Christ says, not what the preacher thinks.

■ A VERSE TO REMEMBER

Now we have received, not the spirit of the world, but the spirit which is of God; that we might know the things that are freely given to us of God.—1 Corinthians 2:12

■ DAILY BIBLE READINGS

Mar. 6 — Proclaiming Christ Crucified. 1 Cor. 2:1–5

The Church and Its Leaders

Basic Passage: 1 Corinthians 4:1–13

Its fun to watch him work. He has been involved in church work for forty years. His resumé reflects a lifetime of accomplishments. None of this is important to this mature pastor. Working among a congregation that has been hurt and split and discouraged, he gently moves from house to house, baseball field to golf course, hospital to funeral home, Bible study group to women's group, senior adults to cradle roll. Each stop leaves a gentle touch of love and encouragement. Each stop brings loyalty back to the church, people back to fellowship with other believers, and a church back to Christ. This is mature leadership.

▓ THE BIBLE LESSON

1 Corinthians 4

1 Let a man so account of us, as of the ministers of Christ, and stewards of the mysteries of God.

2 Moreover it is required in stewards, that a man be found faithful.

3 But with me it is a very small thing that I should be judged of you, or of man's judgment: yea, I judge not mine own self.

4 For I know nothing by myself; yet am I not hereby justified: but he that judgeth me is the Lord.

5 Therefore judge nothing before the time, until the Lord come, who both will bring to light the hidden things of darkness, and will make manifest the counsels of the hearts: and then shall every man have praise of God.

6 And these things, brethren, I have in a figure transferred to myself and to Apollos for your sakes; that ye might learn in us not to think of men above that which is written, that no one of you be puffed up for one against another.

7 For who maketh thee to differ from another? and what hast thou that thou didst not receive? now if thou didst receive it, why dost thou glory, as if thou hadst not received it?

8 Now ye are full, now ye are rich, ye have reigned as kings without us: and I would to God ye did reign, that we also might reign with you.

9 For I think that God hath set forth us the apostles last, as it were appointed to death: for we are made a spectacle unto the world, and to angels, and to men.

10 We are fools for Christ's sake, but ye are wise in Christ; we are weak, but ye are strong; ye are honourable, but we are despised.

11 Even unto this present hour we both hunger, and thirst, and are naked, and are buffeted, and have no certain dwellingplace;

12 And labour, working with our own hands: being reviled, we bless; being persecuted, we suffer it:

13 Being defamed, we intreat: we are made as the filth of the world, and are the offscouring of all things unto this day.

■ THE LESSON EXPLAINED

Judged by God (4:1–5)

Whose opinion matters? Should Apollos have the last word? Or the Jerusalem church represented by Peter? Or should Paul's statement solve the issue? Turn the issue around? Whose word matters to the preacher? Must he please deacons? Elders? Trustees? Teachers? Senior members? Forget all such squabbling. Every church leader has one job description: steward for Jesus. Jesus has planted the Spirit in us. The Spirit gives us the mind of Christ, knowing the mysteries of God's eternal plan of salvation through Christ's death on the cross. I must be faithful to preach what Christ did and what the Spirit says. No one else's opinion must determine what I say or do. Even if I have a clear conscience and think I am doing right, that does not matter. What matters is what God thinks of me and how He will judge me finally. So you get out of the judging business. Quit condemning your preachers. Just be ready to face God when He comes.

Gifted by God (4:6–8)

Now you can apply all this to your wrangling over whether Apollos or I preaches better. The point is not which one of us wins. The point is that you do not become proud on human grounds and start fighting among yourselves over human matters. Whatever you have worth having, you got from God. That means it is all a gift. You deserved nothing. You earned nothing. What do you have to be proud of?

How in the world can you be so self-satisfied? Do you think you have already received all that Christ has to give you? Do you think you are kings ruling over and judging everyone else? Do you think you have become more spiritual than your teachers and earned a rank we have not yet achieved? Oh, that the kingdom had already come, and we had begun our reign with God. That is not the case. You have no reason to boast. Christ showed us what the kingdom is like. We must be faithful stewards, humbly serving Him until He comes back.

Persecuted for God (4:9–13)

Just look at you, so puffed up you think you have already arrived with Christ's wisdom, strength, honor. Better take a look at your leaders. God is letting the world persecute us just as He let them crucify Jesus. The life of strength and riches and glory is not the life of Christ and His disciples. I must warn you of this like a loving father warns his children.

■ TRUTHS TO LIVE BY

God's leaders are faithful stewards. A leader does not glory in what he has or what she accomplishes. A leader does not use a position in the church to exercise personal power and receive personal reward. A leader is a servant, accountable to Christ, and faithful to act and do just as Christ did and as Christ says.

God's leaders are never full of pride. The world teaches us to compete, to climb the ladder, to be successful. Christ teaches us to accept the world's persecution and scorn. We accomplish nothing. Christ gives all we have and accomplishes all we achieve. No reason for pride, ever.

God's leaders are persecuted by the world. Success in the world and congratulations from humans should cause pause for church leaders. The Bible never describes it that way. Doing what Christ wants is doing what the world does not want. Conflict ensues. The world uses its power to harm us. We expect to suffer. Christ did.

▪ A VERSE TO REMEMBER

Let a man so account of us, as of the ministers of Christ, and stewards of the mysteries of God.—1 Corinthians 4:1

▪ DAILY BIBLE READINGS

Mar. 13 — Apollos and Paul, Servants of Christ. 1 Cor. 4:1–7
Mar. 14 — The Ministry of Apostles. 1 Cor. 4:8–13
Mar. 15 — Paul's Fatherly Love for the Corinthians. 1 Cor. 4:14–21
Mar. 16 — Clothe Yourselves with Humility. 1 Pet. 5:1–5
Mar. 17 — Faithful Leaders Will Encounter Suffering. 1 Pet. 5:6–11
Mar. 18 — Do Not Judge One Another. Rom. 14:1–12
Mar. 19 — Live in Harmony with One Another. Rom. 15:1–6

The Need for Discipline in the Church

Basic Passage: 1 Corinthians 5:1–13

A large blank space should fill this introduction to the lesson. My years of ministry have exposed me to most things that go on in a church in one way or another. From all that experience I cannot drum up one example of a church truly exercising loving, responsible discipline on a member, losing persons from membership so the persons would realize the error of their ways, repent, and come back to Christ and the church. Have you seen a church practice such disciplined, loving discipleship? Why?

■ THE BIBLE LESSON

1 Corinthians 5

1 It is reported commonly that there is fornication among you, and such fornication as is not so much as named among the Gentiles, that one should have his father's wife.

2 And ye are puffed up, and have not rather mourned, that he that hath done this deed might be taken away from among you.

3 For I verily, as absent in body, but present in spirit, have judged already, as though I were present, concerning him that hath so done this deed,

4 In the name of our Lord Jesus Christ, when ye are gathered together, and my spirit, with the power of our Lord Jesus Christ,

5 To deliver such an one unto Satan for the destruction of the flesh, that the spirit may be saved in the day of the Lord Jesus.

6 Your glorying is not good. Know ye not that a little leaven leaveneth the whole lump?

7 Purge out therefore the old leaven, that ye may be a new lump, as ye are unleavened. For even Christ our passover is sacrificed for us:

8 Therefore let us keep the feast, not with old leaven, neither with the leaven of malice and wickedness; but with the unleavened bread of sincerity and truth.

9 I wrote unto you in an epistle not to company with fornicators:

10 Yet not altogether with the fornicators of this world, or with the covetous, or extortioners, or with idolaters; for then must ye needs go out of the world.

11 But now I have written unto you not to keep company, if any man that is called a brother be a fornicator, or covetous, or an idolater, or a railer, or a drunkard, or an extortioner; with such an one no not to eat.

12 For what have I to do to judge them also that are without? do not ye judge them that are within?

13 But them that are without God judgeth. Therefore put away from among yourselves that wicked person.

■ THE LESSON EXPLAINED

Ignoring Sin (5:1, 2)

Paul had good sources. They told him explicitly what was happening in Corinth. A man was living in sin with his stepmother. The church in its pride of accomplishment winked at such sinful doings among members. Paul called for immediate action. Go into mourning as a church that your fellowship is such that sin can reign so blatantly in it. Discipline the sinners by taking away their membership in the fellowship. Never ignore sin in the church. The holy God cannot be present in a sinful church.

Disciplining the Sinner (5:3–7)

Paul had no doubt of the right course of action. The church needed to meet, knowing he was present in spirit if not in body and Jesus was present, act in the name of Jesus with Jesus' power. Put the member out of the church. Acknowledge what is already true. Satan controls that person. Jesus does not. Let the person consciously enter the world of the flesh again, separated from Jesus, His worship, His fellowship, and His presence. The person will then learn what he is missing and return fully to Christ so that he will be prepared to participate in the grand salvation at the last day. He must choose life in the flesh with the world or life in the Spirit with Christ.

The church must be careful. If they do not discipline, they will become like the one needing discipline. His sin will infect the whole body just as a little yeast causes the whole loaf of bread to rise. Get rid of this infecting influence in your church. Remember Christ sacrificed Himself for the church, so the church must sacrifice one member for the good of the whole and the good of the member.

Purifying the Church (5:8–13)

Christ was sacrificed on the cross as the Passover Lamb, replacing the Jewish festival celebrating the deliverance from Egypt (Exod. 12). The church celebrates the crucifixion and resurrection as the new festival. The question is the attitude the celebrating church has: self-righteousness or humility; pride or gratitude; truth or fantasy. This is not the first time Paul has warned them. A previous letter now lost told them the same thing. The church must not be seen by the world as represented by sinners. You have to live with the sinners in the world. You cannot tolerate them in the church. Practice church discipline so the church will be pure in the eyes of God and in the eyes of the world. Quit spending all your time condemning what the world does. Let God do that. Get on with your own business. Discipline the sinner in your midst. Make the church pure.

■ TRUTHS TO LIVE BY

The church must show the world Christ's body in pure form. The world sees Christ only as it sees the church. A church that tolerates willful and ongoing sin in its membership is a church that lies to the world. Christ is not like that. We must not be like that.

Sin in the church helps neither the sinner nor the church. Refusing to discipline seems to grant God's grace to the sinner and demonstrate the love and grace of the church. It does neither. It gives the sinner a false security and the church a bad reputation.

Discipline in the church is God's way. Discipline is not a self-righteous act saying we are better than you. Discipline is a recognition that the whole body has failed. Discipline is an attempt to restore the body to be what Christ calls it to be and to restore the sinner to Christ and eternal salvation.

■ A VERSE TO REMEMBER

Therefore let us keep the feast, not with old leaven, neither with the leaven of malice and wickedness; but with the unleavened bread of sincerity and truth.—1 Corinthians 5:8

■ DAILY BIBLE READINGS

Mar. 20 — Sexual Immorality Defiles the Church.
1 Cor. 5:1–8

Mar. 21 — Sexual Immorality Must Be Judged.
1 Cor. 5:9–13

Mar. 22 — Resist Lawsuits among Believers. 1 Cor. 6:1–11

Mar. 23 — Watch Your Tongue. James 3:1–12

Mar. 24 — Choose Wisdom that Is from Above.
James 3:13–18

Mar. 25 — Submit to God's Will and Way. James 4:1–10

Mar. 26 — Seek Humility, and Avoid Judging.
James 4:11–17

Counsel Concerning Marriage

Basic Passage: 1 Corinthians 7:1–5, 8–16

I stand right in the middle of this lesson. I am anxious to see what it teaches me. I experienced thirty years of marriage with a beautiful, intelligent, dedicated Mary. I have been single for two-and-a-half years since cancer claimed her life. One year ago almost to the day that I am writing this, I performed the wedding ceremony for my youngest son and a lovely Kentucky lass. Now I watch as my older son cautiously enters into a relationship with a young woman and as my friends and family constantly question when I am going to give up the single life and get married again. What does God say about life, love, marriage, and the single life?

■ THE BIBLE LESSON

1 Corinthians 7

1 Now concerning the things whereof ye wrote unto me: It is good for a man not to touch a woman.

2 Nevertheless, to avoid fornication, let every man have his own wife, and let every woman have her own husband.

3 Let the husband render unto the wife due benevolence: and likewise also the wife unto the husband.

4 The wife hath not power of her own body, but the husband: and likewise also the husband hath not power of his own body, but the wife.

5 Defraud ye not one the other, except it be with consent for a time, that ye may give yourselves to fasting and prayer; and come together again, that Satan tempt you not for your incontinency.

8 I say therefore to the unmarried and widows, It is good for them if they abide even as I.

9 But if they cannot contain, let them marry: for it is better to marry than to burn.

10 And unto the married I command, yet not I, but the Lord, Let not the wife depart from her husband:

11 But and if she depart, let her remain unmarried, or be reconciled to her husband: and let not the husband put away his wife.

12 But to the rest speak I, not the Lord: If any brother hath a wife that believeth not, and she be pleased to dwell with him, let him not put her away.

13 And the woman which hath an husband that believeth not, and if he be pleased to dwell with her, let her not leave him.

14 For the unbelieving husband is sanctified by the wife, and the unbelieving wife is sanctified by the husband: else were your children unclean; but now are they holy.

15 But if the unbelieving depart, let him depart. A brother or a sister is not under bondage in such cases: but God hath called us to peace.

16 For what knowest thou, O wife, whether thou shalt save thy husband? or how knowest thou, O man, whether thou shalt save thy wife?

■ THE LESSON EXPLAINED

The Marriage Situation (7:1-5, 8, 9)

Paul maintained a correspondence with the Corinthian church (5:9). He wrote to answer questions they raised. Marriage was a hot topic because many thought Christ was coming so soon that people should concentrate on His work rather than bothering with the time-consuming relationship of marriage. Others thought they had already entered the eternal kingdom (4:8) and thus were beyond the bonds of earthly laws and relationships. The Corinthians thus wrote: It is good for a man not to touch a woman.

Paul says, Hey, wait a minute. You know I do not approve of fornication or sexual sin of any kind. Thus, marriage is essential. You must go on with life in the world while you wait for Christ to return. People need to be married. They need to satisfy one another's sexual needs. Each marriage partner dedicates his or her body to meet the needs of the other. Do not cheat your partner. Have the relationship you need unless you agree to abstain for a definite period of time for spiritual reasons. Then return to normal relationships, or Satan will use the temptation to lead you to sinful relationships.

Paul continued: I am giving my own opinion here, an opinion the church subsequently canonized and gave authority to. I am using my own example. I wish every person could be like me and able to control sexual impulses, but this is a spiritual gift from God. If you are not married or if you are a widow or widower, stay unmarried, unless you do not have the gift to do so. If passions burn within you, avoid sin. Enter the normal relationship of marriage.

The Marriage Time (7:10, 11)

Marriage is a lifetime commitment. Do not look for reasons to leave your marriage partner. If you must depart, do not do so for another person. Try to reconcile yourself with the person you separated from. Reconciliation is the church's message and must be the church's example. Here Paul does not just rely on his experience with the Spirit. He can refer back to what Jesus Himself said (Mark 10:11; 5:32; Luke 16:18).

Marriage without Faith (7:12–16)

Paul's teaching on marriage assumes both partners are Christian believers. He has a word for those whose partners are not believers. Maintain the marriage if possible. The believing partner has strong influence for good on the other, giving the unbeliever much more opportunity to find salvation in faith in Christ and providing opportunity for children to become believers. Here holy and sanctified (made holy) are used in a special sense of setting a person apart to special relationship with God so that they have opportunity for faith. Holy in this instance does not mean being morally pure or being saved. Leaving a marriage with an unbeliever may become necessary, but it puts the unbeliever under slavery to sin without the nearness and the holy example of the believer. Do all you can to lead an unsaved marriage partner to God.

■ TRUTHS TO LIVE BY

God approves the single life. Not marrying is not a sin. It is the way Paul lived and approved. It represents possession of a spiritual gift that allows one to live without sexual relationships and serve God.

God approves sexual relationships in marriage. God created man and woman to be together in marriage. Creation expected marriage to be the normal state. People who need sexual relationships should find a marriage partner to love and complete psychologically, spiritually, and physically.

God knows the problems of marriage. Relationships between two people bring misunderstanding, frustration, and anger. These happen. God knows that. These are not reasons to give up. God formed marriage as a lifetime commitment. Keep your commitment, and let God help you and your mate overcome the stresses and misunderstandings of relationship. Never see divorce as the easy way out. It is only a very last resort.

■ A VERSE TO REMEMBER

What? know ye not that your body is the temple of the Holy Ghost which is in you, which ye have of God, and ye are not your own?—1 Corinthians 6:19

■ DAILY BIBLE READINGS

Mar. 27 — Jesus Teaches about Divorce. Mark 10:1–9
Mar. 28 — Strive for Moral Purity. 1 Cor. 6:12–20
Mar. 29 — Be Faithful to Your Spouse. 1 Cor. 7:1–7
Mar. 30 — Directions about Single and Married Life.
            1 Cor. 7:8–16
Mar. 31 — Remain with God above All Else. 1 Cor. 7:17–24
Apr. 1 — Married or Not, the Time is Short. 1 Cor. 7:25–31
Apr. 2 — Does Marriage Hinder Discipleship? 1 Cor. 7:32–40

Concerning Love and Knowledge

Basic Passage: 1 Corinthians 8

Trivial issues divide churches and separate believers. I remember the big issues in my hometown church for young people. Did you go to the senior prom or not? Did you dance or not? Could God possibly have placed dancing feet on the same legs with praying knees? Many young people solved the problem simply. They refused to dance. They did not go to the prom. Instead, they got in the automobile together and went out to the local lake for the evening. What ways we do find to solve moral problems!

■ THE BIBLE LESSON

1 Corinthians 8

1 Now as touching things offered unto idols, we know that we all have knowledge. Knowledge puffeth up, but charity edifieth.

2 And if any man think that he knoweth any thing, he knoweth nothing yet as he ought to know.

3 But if any man love God, the same is known of him.

4 As concerning therefore the eating of those things that are offered in sacrifice unto idols, we know that an idol is nothing in the world, and that there is none other God but one.

5 For though there be that are called gods, whether in heaven or in earth, (as there be gods many, and lords many,)

6 But to us there is but one God, the Father, of whom are all things, and we in him; and one Lord Jesus Christ, by whom are all things, and we by him.

7 Howbeit there is not in every man that knowledge: for some with conscience of the idol unto this hour eat it as a thing offered unto an idol; and their conscience being weak is defiled.

8 But meat commendeth us not to God: for neither, if we eat, are we the better; neither, if we eat not, are we the worse.

9 But take heed lest by any means this liberty of yours become a stumblingblock to them that are weak.

10 For if any man see thee which hast knowledge sit at meat in the idol's temple, shall not the conscience of him which is weak be emboldened to eat those things which are offered to idols;

11 And through thy knowledge shall the weak brother perish, for whom Christ died?

12 But when ye sin so against the brethren, and wound their weak conscience, ye sin against Christ.

13 Wherefore, if meat make my brother to offend, I will eat no flesh while the world standeth, lest I make my brother to offend.

■ THE LESSON EXPLAINED

The Reality: Only One God (8:1–6)

The Corinthians had specific problems. Paul had detailed answers. Do you eat meat that is sacrificed by worshipers of pagan gods, then sold from the temple to the meat market? Does this mean you are approving of idol worship? Does it mean you are eating unclean food? Does it make you unclean and/or unfaithful?

This is an issue of love and knowledge. Do you seek to understand the problem and then solve it intellectually, making yourself proud of your accomplishment? Or do you love people who belong to Christ and want to do what is best for them? We all share one piece of knowledge: idols have no real existence as gods. Only one God exists. Others are fakes. Many people may be fooled and follow other "lords" and worship other "gods." That makes no difference. The gods are still fakes. God the Father created all. Christ the Son provided final salvation. We need no other gods. Knowledge issue settled.

The Problem: Misunderstanding (8:7-9)

Some people cannot put this knowledge into practice. When they eat meat sacrificed to an idol, their consciences begin to ask questions. Now, eating is not the question. We learned long ago in Christ that what we eat does not affect our spiritual status with Christ. In Him nothing is clean or unclean (Acts 10; 11). You are free to eat. You are not free to hurt someone else. Another believer may see you eat and decide the church is not faithful to its principles and so is not to be trusted. If your eating meat causes problems for another, you have two choices. Hold up your freedom and eat. Or hold up your love for the fellowship and do not eat.

The Christian Way: Love Others (8:10-13)

Eating meat sacrificed to idols may lead you to participate with friends in a gathering at a temple where idols are worshiped. It may even lead you to invite the "weak with consciences" to join you. You think you are helping them grow in Christ, overcoming senseless "conscience." Instead, you are destroying them. You are taking them back where they came from—idol worship. You are setting them on the brink of returning to the life from which Jesus called them. Your knowledge, your strength, your lack of conscience, your freedom has led them away from Christ back to idolatry. Proud of yourself? Or is it more important that Christ loved the person enough to die for that person, and you should love that person just as much? Give up your freedom for the sake of loving the other. Not to do so is to sin against Jesus, to renounce His loving death. I will never do anything that threatens the faith of my Christian brother!

■   TRUTHS TO LIVE BY

Superior knowledge does not make you superior. The Christian life is not a contest to see who knows the most, quotes the most Scripture, and has faith to enter into the most activities. The Christian life is love for other people, love that sacrifices my freedom for their good.

False doctrine leads to false practice. This is true for both strong and weak. The strong find freedom and make it the central issue in Christian life. The weak turn morality into legalism and miss the full life Christ offers. Both need to find love as the central issue and become unified in loving and serving Christ.

Teaching through loving action. What you say is drowned out by how you relate. Your teaching and doctrine may be just what Scripture says, but they do little good if you do not practice Christian love, understanding those who do not have your knowledge and doing that which maintains their faith rather than driving them off and back to a life without Christ.

■ A VERSE TO REMEMBER

And if any man think that he knoweth any thing, he knoweth nothing yet as he ought to know. But if any man love God, the same is known of him.—1 Corinthians 8:2,3

■ DAILY BIBLE READINGS

Apr. 3 — Knowledge Puffs Up; Love Builds Up.
1 Cor. 8:1–6
Apr. 4 — Don't Cause Another to Stumble. 1 Cor. 8:7–13
Apr. 5 — Love Has Priority over "Rights." 1 Cor. 9:1–12
Apr. 6 — Preaching the Gospel Is Reward Enough.
1 Cor. 9:13–18
Apr. 7 — Walk Your Talk! 1 Cor. 9:19–27
Apr. 8 — Learn from Lessons of the Past. 1 Cor. 10:1–13
Apr. 9 — Flee from the Worship of Idols. 1 Cor. 10:14–22

Spiritual Gifts

Basic Passage: 1 Corinthians 12:4–20, 26

The subject of the hour. Every church, every conference, every study group wants to know or teach about spiritual gifts. People list their spiritual gifts on Christian resumés. Churches are taking inventories of the spiritual gifts of their members. Everyone's talking about them. The question: Who is exercising them? In many churches a Timothy ministry or something like it is being developed to train people to truly exercise their spiritual gifts and to let the church create openings wherein people may use their gifts.

■ THE BIBLE LESSON

1 Corinthians 12

4 Now there are diversities of gifts, but the same Spirit.

5 And there are differences of administrations, but the same Lord.

6 And there are diversities of operations, but it is the same God which worketh all in all.

7 But the manifestation of the Spirit is given to every man to profit withal.

8 For to one is given by the Spirit the word of wisdom; to another the word of knowledge by the same Spirit;

9 To another faith by the same Spirit; to another the gifts of healing by the same Spirit;

10 To another the working of miracles; to another prophecy; to another discerning of spirits; to another divers kinds of tongues; to another the interpretation of tongues:

11 But all these worketh that one and the selfsame Spirit, dividing to every man severally as he will.

12 For as the body is one, and hath many members, and all the members of that one body, being many, are one body: so also is Christ.

13 For by one Spirit are we all baptized into one body, whether we be Jews or Gentiles, whether we be bond or free; and have been all made to drink into one Spirit.

14 For the body is not one member, but many.

15 If the foot shall say, Because I am not the hand, I am not of the body; is it therefore not of the body?

16 And if the ear shall say, Because I am not the eye, I am not of the body; is it therefore not of the body?

17 If the whole body were an eye, where were the hearing? If the whole were hearing, where were the smelling?

18 But now hath God set the members every one of them in the body, as it hath pleased him.

19 And if they were all one member, where were the body?

20 But now are they many members, yet but one body.

26 And whether one member suffer, all the members suffer with it; or one member be honoured, all the members rejoice with it.

■ THE LESSON EXPLAINED

Gifts Confess Christ (12:1–3)

The Corinthians wrote asking Paul about spiritual gifts, admitting their ignorance. Paul spoke to people who knew they had been taught to worship idols. Now they worshiped Christ, an entirely different lifestyle. You could go from one idol to another. You could curse one idol in the name of another. You could worship more than one idol at a time. Not so with Christ. Christ has given you the Spirit to guide your life. Be sure of one thing. The Spirit will never curse Christ and lead you to another god. The Spirit will always make you say, Jesus is Lord.

Gifts Are All from God (12:4–11)

Gifts come from God's spirit. They come in many kinds. No list suffices to name them all. They lead you to administer or serve God in ministry in various ways. Gifts lead to different results. The same God works through every gift in different persons in different ways. This does not witness to more than one God. It witnesses to God's manifold way of working through His people to achieve His purposes. Gifts will give people wisdom to make decisions, knowledge to teach the church, faith to trust God and do what He commands, power to heal, ability to do miracles, understanding to explain God's ways, capability to know what God's Spirit is saying amidst the confusion of many voices, skill to speak foreign languages or unknown tongues, and ability to interpret what those speaking in tongues say. Every gift the Spirit gives. Every gift the Spirit uses for His purposes. Let the Spirit do His work the way He chooses. Do not try to change the Spirit or get the gift you think is best.

Gifts Are All for One Church (12:12–20, 26)

You have one Lord, Jesus Christ. He gave you one spirit—the Holy Spirit. He gathered many people into one body—the church. We had to meet no particular qualifications of race, background, religion, knowledge. God chose who would believe and be baptized into the church and receive the Spirit. Every member God chose is important. God's church needs every one, just as the human body needs every body part. God created the human body so it functions just like He wants. He created His body, the church, with all its members so it functions just as He wants. He does not create individuals to do their thing. He crafts them all into one unified body. We are not competing for honors against one another. We cooperate and empathize and suffer and serve together. Honors come. We share. Problems come. We share. We are one. Gifts unite. They do not divide. Gifts serve and honor God. They do not determine who is best.

■ TRUTHS TO LIVE BY

God's gifts lead you to honor Christ. Christ's Spirit has given you one or more gifts. You have one purpose with these gifts: Honor Christ. Any time you use the gift to gain self-importance or power, you have misused the gift. The gift seeks honor only for Jesus.

God's gifts never make you more important than someone else. Gifts are not for your benefit. They are for Christ's benefit. Gifts never separate one individual or group out as more valuable to the church than others. God does not have a job rating scale that determines how much you should be rewarded by the gift you have.

God's gifts always serve the church. Spiritual gifts never single out the individual for attention. Gifts bring the church together in ministry and service. Gifts enable the church to be and do what Christ wants His body to be and do in the world for which He died.

■ A VERSE TO REMEMBER

Now there are diversities of gifts, but the same Spirit. And there are differences of administrations, but the same Lord. And there are diversities of operations, but it is the same God which worketh all in all.—1 Corinthians 12:4-6

■ DAILY BIBLE READINGS

Apr. 10 — Understand the Source of Spiritual Gifts.
          1 Cor. 12:1-6
Apr. 11 — Many Spiritual Gifts, but One Spirit.
          1 Cor. 12:7-11
Apr. 12 — One Body, Many Members. 1 Cor. 12:12-20
Apr. 13 — We Need One Another. 1 Cor. 12:21-31
Apr. 14 — Transformed by New Life in Christ.
          Rom. 12:1-8
Apr. 15 — Marks of a Faithful Christian. Rom. 12:9-15
Apr. 16 — Guidance for Living the Christian Life.
          Rom. 12:16-21

Christ's Resurrection and Ours

Basic Passage: 1 Corinthians 15:20–27, 35–44

Walking the dirt lanes of Kenya with faithful brothers and sisters in Christ often brought one fateful question: How is life different in America than here in Kenya? No answer sufficed for such a question. Here is one I always try to give. Life is very similar in both places for us because we have the assurance of resurrection. No matter what life is like now, one day we will join together to praise Christ in heaven. Whatever conditions and circumstances may be different, one constant unites: the hope of the resurrection. This is what makes Christianity unique. Surely we must do our best to understand it, teach it, live it.

◼ THE BIBLE LESSON

1 Corinthians 15

20 But now is Christ risen from the dead, and become the firstfruits of them that slept.

21 For since by man came death, by man came also the resurrection of the dead.

22 For as in Adam all die, even so in Christ shall all be made alive.

23 But every man in his own order: Christ the firstfruits; afterward they that are Christ's at his coming.

24 Then cometh the end, when he shall have delivered up the kingdom to God, even the Father; when he shall have put down all rule and all authority and power.

25 For he must reign, till he hath put all enemies under his feet.

26 The last enemy that shall be destroyed is death.

27 For he hath put all things under his feet. But when he saith all things are put under him, it is manifest that he is excepted, which did put all things under him.

35 But some man will say, How are the dead raised up? and with what body do they come?

36 Thou fool, that which thou sowest is not quickened, except it die:

37 And that which thou sowest, thou sowest not that body that shall be, but bare grain, it may chance of wheat, or of some other grain:

38 But God giveth it a body as it hath pleased him, and to every seed his own body.

39 All flesh is not the same flesh: but there is one kind of flesh of men, another flesh of beasts, another of fishes, and another of birds.

40 There are also celestial bodies, and bodies terrestrial: but the glory of the celestial is one, and the glory of the terrestrial is another.

41 There is one glory of the sun, and another glory of the moon, and another glory of the stars: for one star differeth from another star in glory.

42 So also is the resurrection of the dead. It is sown in corruption; it is raised in incorruption:

43 It is sown in dishonour; it is raised in glory: it is sown in weakness; it is raised in power:

44 It is sown a natural body; it is raised a spiritual body. There is a natural body, and there is a spiritual body.

■ THE LESSON EXPLAINED

The First Resurrection (15:20–23)

Christian faith stands or falls on the resurrection of Christ. It determines whether we are fools or the only truth-knowing, truth-believing people in history. It determines whether we have to face death without hope, leave the unjust world as the final reality, and seek reincarnation or absorption into the All as the ultimate destiny of life. We proclaim Christ was raised. That means we will also be raised from death. Adam's sin spelled death for every other person ever born. Christ's resurrection offers hope to every person who will believe and trust in that resurrection. Resurrection is not immediate, not something that has already occurred. Only Christ's resurrection is a fact of history. The rest of us must wait until He comes again.

The Resurrection Kingdom (15:24–27)

Christ came preaching the presence of the kingdom of God in His ministry (Mark 1:15). That kingdom will be fully visible and in power over all the earth one day when Christ comes again. He will destroy all governments, all institutions, and all spiritual powers including Satan, who would oppose His kingdom. Even the power of death will be ended. After Christ comes, no more marriage. No more births. No more deaths. Either eternal life or eternal punishment. Then He will tell the Father, It is now finished. The kingdom is come on earth as in heaven. Here, I give you the kingdom back. The entire earth will know Christ is king, but for most it will be too late. They will not have opportunity to repent and be part of the kingdom. They will have rejected Christ once and forever.

The Resurrection Body (15:35–44)

Talking of resurrection raises questions. What will we look like? Who will we know? Paul tries to answer a few. First, all must die. Just as in the world of planting seed and reaping grain, so we must plant the dead body in the grave before we can have the resurrection body. God has designed each body for each person and each animal as He chose. He has also chosen to give a different kind of prominence, honor, glory. We see this by comparing the grandeur of the sun, moon, and stars with our own earthly grandeur.

Just as God created all these differences, so He has created another difference: between the body we have on earth and the one we have in heaven. The earthly body is temporary, subject to suffering and scarring and sin. The earthly body is physical, and it dies. The resurrection body we will receive is spiritual and will never die. But we cannot be raised as bodiless spirits. We must have the resurrection body, the perfect gift God has prepared for us for eternity.

TRUTHS TO LIVE BY

Christ's resurrection insures your resurrection. Death is your future. Beyond death you have no future, unless someone gives it to you. Christ died and was raised from the dead. He gives you hope. As God raised Christ, making the tomb empty, so He will raise you.

Christ's resurrection insures the kingdom's coming. You have no kingdom if you have only a dead king. Christ lives. His kingdom is coming. All other powers and rulers will vanish. Christ will rule over everything and everyone except for God the Father. Christ will hand the kingdom to Him for eternity.

Christ's resurrection reveals the resurrection body. Some questions Scripture does not answer. One is the exact nature of the resurrection body. It does give us one major source of certainty. Christ had a glorious resurrection body that could do miracles and overcome the rules of earthly existence. We will have a resurrection body like His.

A VERSE TO REMEMBER

But now is Christ risen from the dead, and become the firstfruits of them that slept. For since by man came death, by man came also the resurrection of the dead. For as in Adam all die, even so in Christ shall all be made alive.
—1 Corinthians 15:20–22

DAILY BIBLE READINGS

Apr. 17 — The Resurrection of Christ the Lord. 1 Cor. 15:1–11
Apr. 18 — How Can You Deny the Resurrection?
　　　　　　1 Cor. 15:12–19
Apr. 19 — The Resurrected Christ Destroys Death.
　　　　　　1 Cor. 15:20–28
Apr. 20 — The Dead Are Raised: Believe It.
　　　　　　1 Cor. 15:29–34
Apr. 21 — God Will Give the Glory. 1 Cor. 15:35–41
Apr. 22 — Raised the Spiritual Body. 1 Cor. 15:42–49
Apr. 23 — We Have a Victory through Jesus Christ.
　　　　　　1 Cor. 15:50–58

The Way of Love

Basic Passage: 1 Corinthians 12:31–13:13

What a vantage point from which to study this lesson! A newlywed son and daughter-in-law seeking to establish their own love nest. Another son just entering a relationship wondering if it will lead to love. And myself looking back over thirty years with a now-deceased wife and looking forward wondering if a new relationship will lead again to love. Meanwhile, another kind of love binds me to friends from college, from seminary, from teaching days in Atlanta, from pastoring days, and from European days. Every relationship is different. Each teaches me something new about love. All fall short of the love Christ taught Paul to describe as the greatest experience of our world.

■ **THE BIBLE LESSON**

1 Corinthians 12

31 But covet earnestly the best gifts: and yet shew I unto you a more excellent way.

. . . .

1 Corinthians 13

1 Though I speak with the tongues of men and of angels, and have not charity, I am become as sounding brass, or a tinkling cymbal.

2 And though I have the gift of prophecy, and understand all mysteries, and all knowledge; and though I have all faith, so that I could remove mountains, and have not charity, I am nothing.

3 And though I bestow all my goods to feed the poor, and though I give my body to be burned, and have not charity, it profiteth me nothing.

4 Charity suffereth long, and is kind; charity envieth not; charity vaunteth not itself, is not puffed up,

5 Doth not behave itself unseemly, seeketh not her own, is not easily provoked, thinketh no evil;

6 Rejoiceth not in iniquity, but rejoiceth in the truth;

7 Beareth all things, believeth all things, hopeth all things, endureth all things.

8 Charity never faileth: but whether there be prophecies, they shall fail; whether there be tongues, they shall cease; whether there be knowledge, it shall vanish away.

9 For we know in part, and we prophesy in part.

10 But when that which is perfect is come, then that which is in part shall be done away.

11 When I was a child, I spake as a child, I understood as a child, I thought as a child: but when I became a man, I put away childish things.

12 For now we see through a glass, darkly; but then face to face: now I know in part; but then shall I know even as also I am known.

13 And now abideth faith, hope, charity, these three; but the greatest of these is charity.

■ THE LESSON EXPLAINED

Love: The More Excellent Way (12:31–13:3)

A chapter devoted to spiritual gifts led naturally to a question. Which is the best gift? Which does the church the most good? Prophecy? Tongues? Miracles?

You are right to want to have the best gift. Now let's find what it is, the most excellent way of life on earth. It is the way of *agape*, self-giving love. It is better than any tongue-speaking I could do. Even better than the angels can do. It is better than being able to tell people what God expects and what He is going to do. Better than knowing His purposes in a deeper way than anyone else. Better than being a master of biblical teachings. Better than having the greatest amount of faith, enough to tell Mount Everest to move to Africa. Better than caring enough for the poorest people to give them everything I own.

Better than letting the government burn my body rather than giving up my testimony for Christ. No matter what gift I have from God, it is useless if not exercised with love for God, church members, and the world.

Love: Humble and Enduring (13:4–7)

Love suffers in this world but still shows kindness to those who cause the suffering. Love never wants what someone else enjoys. Love never seeks to enhance its own reputation. Is never proud or conceited. Never acts in unchristian ways. Never seeks selfish goals at the expense of others. Never lets someone else prod you into an angry, stupid act. Never occupies your mind with wicked thoughts or plans to hurt others. Never takes pleasure in sinful actions or in harm coming to another. Always loves and rejoices when the truth wins out. Always endures what comes your way without complaint. Always maintains faith and hope in Christ and His promises, no matter what the world throws at you.

Love: Above All (13:8–13)

Love is consistent, not here today and gone tomorrow. Other spiritual gifts finally vanish, no longer useful to God and His church. Such gifts are never perfect, only partially fulfilling God's purpose, always hindered by human imperfection and human incompleteness. Such gifts doing partial service will vanish. Compare it to me growing up. Certain things marked me as a child. When I grew up, I changed. I left childish ways and habits behind.

Same thing with gifts. We use them in a world where we cannot see things plainly. The day is coming when Christ returns, and we are with Him and know all things as He knows all things. Right now most of all we need faith in Christ because we cannot see clearly; we need hope for the future as we endure the present; and we need love for each other and for Christ. Then we shall see and not need faith. We shall know and not have to hope; but we shall still need to love. Love endures even in eternity. Therefore, the greatest of these, the more excellent way, is love!

■ TRUTHS TO LIVE BY

Love is God's best gift. Love is the gift we will still exercise in eternity. Love is the gift of relationship that leads us to exercise all other gifts wisely and properly. Love lifts us above the world to be Godlike. Thus, love is God's best gift.

Love looks to others, not self. Most spiritual gifts can be exercised to our own benefit. We gain confidence, honor, reputation, power, and authority through them. Love always points us away from self toward others. Love makes us be Christlike, taking up a cross and giving our lives for others. Thus, love is best.

Love, not knowledge, mirrors Christ. Even Christ on earth said some knowledge was limited to the Father. Christ attacked the Pharisees and other religious leaders for being able to answer questions but not being able to put the questions into action in life. Love moves knowledge from a source of pride and reputation to a source of good for the world and for God.

■ A VERSE TO REMEMBER

And now abideth faith, hope, charity, these three; but the greatest of these is charity.—1 Corinthians 13:13

■ DAILY BIBLE READINGS

Apr. 24 — The Gift of Love. 1 Cor. 13:1–7
Apr. 25 — Love Is the Greatest Gift of All. 1 Cor. 13:8–13
Apr. 26 — Love: An Old New Commandment.
　　　　　1 John 2:7–17
Apr. 27 — Show Your Love for One Another. 1 John 3:11–17
Apr. 28 — Believe in Jesus, and Love One Another.
　　　　　1 John 3:18–24
Apr. 29 — Let Us Love as God Loves. 1 John 4:7–12
Apr. 30 — We Abide in God If We Love. 1 John 4:13–21

The Christian March of Triumph

Basic Passage: 2 Corinthians 2:4–17

Every parent knows the feeling. Child does wrong. No matter how old the child, you as a parent feel obligated to show the child the error of his or her ways. Then you fret over whether you went too far, punished too severely, broke off relationships with your child for now and forever. Will he ever love you again?

Paul had a similar relationship with the church at Corinth. An individual, quite possibly a member of the church but not necessarily, had criticized Paul openly and vehemently (see ch. 7 for further details of the relationship). Paul wrote a letter severely criticizing the church for not disciplining his accuser. Then Paul began the round of self-questioning. So he wrote this chapter of 2 Corinthians to explain his letter and to help the church on the next step in this relationship. Could they tread the path from sorrow to joy, from discipline to love?

■ **THE BIBLE LESSON**

2 Corinthians 2

4 For out of much affliction and anguish of heart I wrote unto you with many tears; not that ye should be grieved, but that ye might know the love which I have more abundantly unto you.

5 But if any have caused grief, he hath not grieved me, but in part: that I may not overcharge you all.

6 Sufficient to such a man is this punishment, which was inflicted of many.

7 So that contrariwise ye ought rather to forgive him, and comfort him, lest perhaps such a one should be swallowed up with overmuch sorrow.

8 Wherefore I beseech you that ye would confirm your love toward him.

9 For to this end also did I write, that I might know the proof of you, whether ye be obedient in all things.

10 To whom ye forgive any thing, I forgive also: for if I forgave any thing, to whom I forgave it, for your sakes forgave I it in the person of Christ;

11 Lest Satan should get an advantage of us: for we are not ignorant of his devices.

12 Furthermore, when I came to Troas to preach Christ's gospel, and a door was opened unto me of the Lord,

13 I had no rest in my spirit, because I found not Titus my brother: but taking my leave of them, I went from thence into Macedonia.

14 Now thanks be unto God, which always causeth us to triumph in Christ, and maketh manifest the savour of his knowledge by us in every place.

15 For we are unto God a sweet savour of Christ, in them that are saved, and in them that perish:

16 To the one we are the savour of death unto death; and to the other the savour of life unto life. And who is sufficient for these things?

17 For we are not as many, which corrupt the word of God: but as of sincerity, but as of God, in the sight of God speak we in Christ.

■ THE LESSON EXPLAINED

Love Forgives (2:4–11)

Paul wrote a tough love letter to the Corinthians that has been lost in the pages of history (compare 1 Cor. 5:9). The scroll was wet with his tears. A soft heart produced harsh words as he tried to get the Corinthians to deal with someone who accused Paul and caused grief in the church. Paul wrote not to make the church angry, as some accused him, but to show his love and his desire for the church to be what God wanted it to be.

Paul's accuser caused problems for Paul and for the rest of the church. Finally, the church punished him and placed Paul in a strange situation. Punishment time is over. Forgive and forget. Let's restore fellowship if at all possible. You have carried out discipline. Now finish the job. Show your love for the one you disciplined. Do not let him get so caught up in your punishment that he feels isolated from the church and from God. Bring him back to the fold. Restore the wandering sheep. Forgive, forget, and love. Punishment time is over. Reconciliation time is here.

I wrote to see if you would obey the word I sent. You passed the test. You obeyed. Now it is time to start in a new direction. Forgiveness is the key word of the hour. You forgive him, and be certain I will too. I have taken this to Christ and told the Lord I would forgive the man. Forgiveness is essential, or Satan will win the victory. You know how clever Satan is. Watch out. Don't let him win. Forgive.

The Aroma of the Gospel (2:12–17)

Well and good, Paul, said the Corinthians, but what about your promise to come see us again (1:23–2:3). I went to Troas and found God opened the door to evangelism, so I preached there. You know Troas is the port city ten miles south of Troy on the Aegean Sea in northwest Asia (see Acts 16:8, 11; 20:5, 6; 2 Tim. 4:13). From there I launched my first mission to Macedonia and Europe. Quickly, however, I left Troas, because I was worried about you and how you would react to my letter, and Titus had not come to report to me. So I crossed the Aegean into Macedonia again to find him.

Thank God. He always gives us the victory. He lets us smell the glorious aroma of His presence everywhere we go. Thank Him that He considers us a sweet smell in this world of saved and unsaved people. The saved think the aroma of our presence indicates life and hope. Those who have not accepted Christ experience us as the stench of death. Not one of us—you at Corinth or me—is up to the assignment God gives us. I cannot play a role and use the Word of God for my own schemes and purposes as some do. I cannot sell the Word of God to the highest bidder. No, I must be sincere and true in using God's Word. If it says you are doing wrong, I must let you know even when it grieves my heart, for I know God will eventually use it to bring you back to His ways. I can speak only what Christ in me would say to you.

▌ TRUTHS TO LIVE BY

Forgiveness is the Christian way in broken relationships. Broken relationships bring grief and hurt. The temptation is to ignore the relationship and go on to other ones. Scripture says, you must never forget the relationship. You must forgive and do everything possible to reconcile.

Love suffers when other believers suffer. Your advice and Christian counsel may bring suffering to others as they carry it out. You may see situations and circumstances cause others suffering. A disciple of Christ can never watch such situations without passion. We suffer when others suffer. We feel their pain.

Christian practice leads to gospel victory. The easy way out is to find what the majority wants and do it. Christ's way is to discipline, forgive, and love. The majority way limits the fellowship to those who always agree with us, an ever-declining figure. Christ's way of forgiveness, reconciliation, and love becomes evermore inclusive, brings gospel victory to broken lives, and defeats Satan before he can use his wiles and schemes.

▌ A VERSE TO REMEMBER

Now thanks be unto God, which always causeth us to triumph in Christ, and maketh manifest the savour of his knowledge by us in every place.—2 Corinthians 2:14

▌ DAILY BIBLE READINGS

May 1   — God Consoles Us in Our Afflictions. 2 Cor. 1:1–11
May 2   — Sealed by God's Spirit. 2 Cor. 1:12–22
May 3   — Love Prevails over Pain and Conflict. 2 Cor. 1:23–2:4
May 4   — Christian Forgiveness for the Offender. 2 Cor. 2:5–11
May 5   — The Gospel: The Fragrance of Life. 2 Cor. 2:12–17
May 6   — Good News Written on Human Hearts. 2 Cor. 3:1–11
May 7   — Freed and Transformed by the Spirit. 2 Cor. 3:12–18

Trials and Triumphs of Christian Ministry

Basic Passage: 2 Corinthians 4:5–18

Preaching the gospel has challenged me since the first sermon I preached as a young teenager in First Baptist Church of Sweetwater, Texas. I have preached in many states, in Europe, Israel, and Africa. I have preached in famous cathedrals and in open-air meetings without seats for the preacher or the congregation. Blacks, Hispanics, Asians, Africans, Americans, Europeans . . . so many different people have let me preach God's Word to them.

No two preaching sessions have been the same. Many have brought great joy as I shared good news. Others have brought tears and hurt and soul-searching as I have issued the prophetic call for judgment and justice and reconciliation. Gospel preaching moves the preacher from suffering to triumph. Paul found this so, and so have the centuries of preachers who have followed him.

■ THE BIBLE LESSON

2 Corinthians 4

5 For we preach not ourselves, but Christ Jesus the Lord; and ourselves your servants for Jesus' sake.

6 For God, who commanded the light to shine out of darkness, hath shined in our hearts, to give the light of the knowledge of the glory of God in the face of Jesus Christ.

7 But we have this treasure in earthen vessels, that the excellency of the power may be of God, and not of us.

8 We are troubled on every side, yet not distressed; we are perplexed, but not in despair;

9 Persecuted, but not forsaken; cast down, but not destroyed;

10 *Always bearing about in the body the dying of the Lord Jesus, that the life also of Jesus might be made manifest in our body.*

11 *For we which live are alway delivered unto death for Jesus' sake, that the life also of Jesus might be made manifest in our mortal flesh.*

12 *So then death worketh in us, but life in you.*

13 *We having the same spirit of faith, according as it is written, I believed, and therefore have I spoken; we also believe, and therefore speak;*

14 *Knowing that he which raised up the Lord Jesus shall raise up us also by Jesus, and shall present us with you.*

15 *For all things are for your sakes, that the abundant grace might through the thanksgiving of many redound to the glory of God.*

16 *For which cause we faint not; but though our outward man perish, yet the inward man is renewed day by day.*

17 *For our light affliction, which is but for a moment, worketh for us a far more exceeding and eternal weight of glory;*

18 *While we look not at the things which are seen, but at the things which are not seen: for the things which are seen are temporal; but the things which are not seen are eternal.*

■ THE LESSON EXPLAINED

Christ: The Topic of Preaching (4:5–7)

Churches face so many decisions because preachers preach to them in so many different ways. The church at Corinth knew messages from Paul, Apollos, Titus, Timothy, Peter and the Jerusalem church, and who knows how many others. All that preaching got confusing. Paul tried to set them on the right track about the nature of preaching. Preaching never centers on the preacher, his intelligence, his humor, his power, his results, his claim to fame. Preaching has one theme: Jesus Christ and Him crucified. Do not see the preacher as anything special. The preacher is only a slave of Jesus. Listen to hear about Jesus, not about the preacher.

God the Creator has created His most magnificent reality: Jesus Christ. In Jesus we see the brilliant flashing light of God's glory. Why preach anything else when preaching Jesus reveals God? Don't think this revelation comes because of human eloquence and power with language. Only God can make it happen. The preacher is a clay flowerpot, quickly and easily broken to pieces. The power is God's.

Suffering: The Results of Preaching (4:8–12)

Preaching is not easy. People say all sorts of things about the preacher. They do all sorts of things to the preacher. The preacher has to wrestle with God, with His Word, and with the consequences of preaching that Word. Preaching the Word brings suffering, but suffering does not make us quit. Despair, hopelessness, all the dark feelings threaten the preacher but never gain victory. Just as Jesus died, so the preacher's body shows marks of suffering and persecution that lead to the brink of death. We gladly suffer even this so that you may know about Jesus and so you may have the eternal life He gives. Our suffering even unto death is worth it all because you have life.

Eternity: The Goal of Preaching (4:13–18)

Psalm 116:10 gave Paul his testimony: I have the same faith as the psalmist—I believe and therefore I speak. My faith means nothing can shut my mouth. God raised Jesus from the dead. He will do the same for us. That is reason enough to testify to everyone who will listen, no matter the earthly consequences. Everything we do, everything we say is for your benefit. We want all to experience the abundant grace of God unto salvation. We want them all to praise God with thanksgiving. We want everything that comes out of our preaching to lead people to give glory and honor and praise to God. If that happens, whatever we suffer is worth it.

We may look weak externally because of all we endure. Never fear. God is renewing us day by day internally. Suffering and persecution lasts for a few minutes. The results will be an eternity of reward, giving God glory forever. Eternal reward is worth momentary troubles. You pay too much attention to what your eyes can see. Don't bother about our physical appearance. Turn on eyes of faith. Look to eternity. See what we have there. Don't worry about the small problems we have here because we preach the gospel. The gospel promises eternal salvation. Nothing else matters.

■ TRUTHS TO LIVE BY

Jesus is always the center of the gospel. People easily slip into the habit of making self the topic of preaching, so that "I" occurs more often in sermons than "Jesus." Biblical preaching always points everyone to Jesus.

Jesus does not protect His servants from trouble. Faithful preaching does not promise uneventful living. Faithful preaching raises anger and ire among the listeners. They often take it out on the preacher. Preachers must suffer the consequences of faithfulness to the truth even as Jesus did.

Jesus promises eternal life to faithful believers. Earthly consequences are unimportant to the preacher. Faithfulness to Christ is all-important, because faithfulness to Him brings eternal life, the goal of preaching.

■ A VERSE TO REMEMBER

We are troubled on every side, yet not distressed; we are perplexed, but not in despair; Persecuted, but not forsaken; cast down, but not destroyed.—2 Corinthians 4:8, 9

■ DAILY BIBLE READINGS

May 8 — God's Light Shines in Our Hearts. 2 Cor. 4:1–7
May 9 — God Raised Jesus and Will Raise Us.
2 Cor. 4:8–15

The Collection for Jerusalem Churches

Basic Passage: 2 Corinthians 9:1–13

Just last week the phone rang. Trent, we are having a problem. We are new at this tithing business. How do we figure out how much to give? the new deacon asked. Two days later, an E-mail appeared on the screen. His wife asked the same question from a different perspective. Today's complicated business setups with people paying more and more of their personal business expenses leads to many serious questions about how to figure the tithe. The happy note is that people are wanting to tithe. This shows maturity in Christ and obedience to His way of life. Hopefully, it also shows utmost gratitude to God, the giver of all we have.

■ THE BIBLE LESSON

2 Corinthians 9

1 For as touching the ministering to the saints, it is superfluous for me to write to you:

2 For I know the forwardness of your mind, for which I boast of you to them of Macedonia, that Achaia was ready a year ago; and your zeal hath provoked very many.

3 Yet have I sent the brethren, lest our boasting of you should be in vain in this behalf; that, as I said, ye may be ready:

4 Lest haply if they of Macedonia come with me, and find you unprepared, we (that we say not, ye) should be ashamed in this same confident boasting.

5 Therefore I thought it necessary to exhort the brethren, that they would go before unto you, and make up beforehand your bounty, whereof ye had notice before, that the same might be ready, as a matter of bounty, and not as of covetousness.

6 But this I say, He which soweth sparingly shall reap also sparingly; and he which soweth bountifully shall reap also bountifully.

7 Every man according as he purposeth in his heart, so let him give; not grudgingly, or of necessity: for God loveth a cheerful giver.

8 And God is able to make all grace abound toward you; that ye, always having all sufficiency in all things, may abound to every good work:

9 (As it is written, He hath dispersed abroad; he hath given to the poor: his righteousness remaineth for ever.

10 Now he that ministereth seed to the sower both minister bread for your food, and multiply your seed sown, and increase the fruits of your righteousness;)

11 Being enriched in every thing to all bountifulness, which causeth through us thanksgiving to God.

12 For the administration of this service not only supplieth the want of the saints, but is abundant also by many thanksgivings unto God;

13 Whiles by the experiment of this ministration they glorify God for your professed subjection unto the gospel of Christ, and for your liberal distribution unto them, and unto all men.

■ THE LESSON EXPLAINED

The Example of Giving (9:1–5)

Finally, something they agree on. Who would think after all the trouble Paul had with Corinth that they could agree on the principles and practices of Christian stewardship, giving, and money management? Corinth was his prime example as he preached to others. He wanted to collect money for the poor people in the persecuted church at Jerusalem, the First Church. Your example has led the other churches I preach to. They want to give, too. But I want to have more reason to boast. You have indicated you want to give. The time has come. The collection committee is on the way. Open up your pockets now and give. Don't embarrass me as I bring these people to whom I have been preaching to see you and to see your fine example of giving. I am giving you advanced warning so you will be ready when the committee gets there. Now you can have the money ready when they come.

The Principle of Giving (9:6–9)

You have heard the old saying: he who sows sparingly will reap sparingly, and he who sows bountifully will reap bountifully. The saying is true. It is time for you to sow your gifts to another church. Will you sow bountifully? Don't let me put a guilt trip on you, however. Your motive is more important than your gift. What does your heart say? God loves a person who gives out of a cheerful heart. Do not feel a grudge against me, thinking I forced you to give. Don't feel like you have to do it because everyone else is. God can give you all you need. Trust Him. Take what He gives you and give to others. Remember Psalm 112:9.

The Purpose of Giving (9:10–13)

Now you know God who provides seed for the farmer and the results of the farmer's labor: bread for us to eat. He will also multiply your resources so you can give liberally. Then He will multiply the results of your giving so your righteous acts may accomplish much for His kingdom. As God gives you resources and as you share these with others, we give thanks to God for all He is doing with and through you. Thus, your giving has two results. It brings much needed help to the very poor people in Jerusalem. It also causes many people to give thanks and praise to God.

To sum up, this is a test for you. When you give generously with a cheerful and thankful heart, others see that your confession of faith in Christ is really true. Thus, because of your faithfulness in giving and in being what you say you are, they glorify God.

■ TRUTHS TO LIVE BY

God's love produces cheerful givers. God's love sent Jesus to die for us. We respond to that love by giving from our resources so others may have what they need and may experience love through us from God. This love atmosphere is one of cheer and gladness, not duty and grudges.

Cheerful givers give abundant gifts. Cheerful givers do not count pennies and see if they meet the minimum requirement. Cheerful givers know God gave His all, and so we give our all to Him and for Him.

Abundant gifts produce thanksgiving and glory for God. Our gifts meet the needs of others. They see Christ in action in us and so praise God. As we give, God gets the glory. Could we ask for anything better to happen?

■ A VERSE TO REMEMBER

Every man according as he purposeth in his heart, so let him give; not grudgingly, or of necessity: for God loveth a cheerful giver.—2 Corinthians 9:7

■ DAILY BIBLE READINGS

May 15 — An Unexpected Example of Generosity. 2 Cor. 8:1–7
May 16 — Show Your Love by Your Giving. 2 Cor. 8:8–15
May 17 — A Generous Gift Glorifies God. 2 Cor. 8:16–24
May 18 — God Loves and Blesses Cheerful Givers.
        2 Cor. 9:1–9
May 19 — Generous Giving Brings Joy to All.
        2 Cor. 9:10–15
May 20 — A Collection for Jerusalem Christians.
        1 Cor. 16:1–9
May 21 — Paul Intends to Visit Roman Christians.
        Rom. 15:22–29

Living in the Faith

Basic Passage: 2 Corinthians 13:1–13

Carefully I studied God's Word and preached and talked and counseled and listened. Thought I had done everything Wayne Oates taught me in pastoral counseling and others showed me about church administration. Now I slowly walked to the church. Time to vote on this issue which I just knew the church had to approve if it were to be the church God wanted it to be. This would help this small traditional church mature and start growing again. The vote matured me, if not the church. Years later, the chairman of the deacons told me I was right and he was wrong. He, too, gradually matured.

Paul faced a third visit to Corinth, knowing it was a test of his leadership in that church. Would this be as painful as a previous visit had been? Would he fail now as he had failed then? (2:1).

■ THE BIBLE LESSON

2 Corinthians 13

1 This is the third time I am coming to you. In the mouth of two or three witnesses shall every word be established.

2 I told you before, and foretell you, as if I were present, the second time; and being absent now I write to them which heretofore have sinned, and to all other, that, if I come again, I will not spare:

3 Since ye seek a proof of Christ speaking in me, which to you–ward is not weak, but is mighty in you.

4 For though he was crucified through weakness, yet he liveth by the power of God. For we also are weak in him, but we shall live with him by the power of God toward you.

5 Examine yourselves, whether ye be in the faith; prove your own selves. Know ye not your own selves, how that Jesus Christ is in you, except ye be reprobates?

6 But I trust that ye shall know that we are not reprobates.

7 Now I pray to God that ye do no evil; not that we should appear approved, but that ye should do that which is honest, though we be as reprobates.

8 For we can do nothing against the truth, but for the truth.

9 For we are glad, when we are weak, and ye are strong: and this also we wish, even your perfection.

10 Therefore I write these things being absent, lest being present I should use sharpness, according to the power which the Lord hath given me to edification, and not to destruction.

11 Finally, brethren, farewell. Be perfect, be of good comfort, be of one mind, live in peace; and the God of love and peace shall be with you.

12 Greet one another with an holy kiss.

13 All the saints salute you.

■ THE LESSON EXPLAINED

Weak with God's Power (13:1–4)

Paul prepared himself and the Corinthian church for his coming. He knew now how they would react to the strong statements and expectations he had stated in this second letter. He reminded them that the word of one idle gossiper did not suffice. They needed two or three witnesses to prove charges against him and against one another (see Num. 35:30; Deut. 17:6). Paul went back almost to where he started his Corinthian correspondence (1 Cor. 5). Sin in the church must be dealt with. Church discipline must be enforced.

You at Corinth really want to discipline me, Paul said. You think I am too meek and mild, not charismatic and showy enough among you. You want proof that Christ speaks through my weak voice. Look at Christ. He is not weak among you. You know the power of the salvation He has brought to you. Look at His life, so weak the Roman government crucified Him on a criminal's cross. God showed how weak that was. God raised Him from the dead and made the cross the central point of your salvation from sin. We are like Christ. We appear to be weak, but God's power works in us. He gives us the power to serve Him. In our humanity we call it weakness God calls it our role as servants.

Lifting Up, Not Tearing Down (13:5–10)

Let's put the light on you. Examine yourselves. Are you passing Christ's test of faith? Is He alive in you? Now can you look at me differently? Do you really think I fail Christ's test? I pray that you will not do wrong. This is not a selfish prayer, wanting you to agree with me and approve my ministry instead of someone else's. I want you to be justified in God's sight, no matter what happens to me or how you judge me. My concern is for the truth, the whole truth, and nothing but the truth.

Believe me. I am happy when you are strong, even if that means I have to appear weak and helpless. We have this one goal for you: we want you to mature and become perfect in the faith of Jesus Christ. I could wait until I come to write these things. Then I would really cause contention and strife among you. So I write now to avoid sharpness later. God has given me power, no matter how weak you think I am. That power is to instruct and build you up, not power to destroy you. Remember, our goal is to bring unity to the church and glory to God, not to destroy the church.

Unity in God's Love and Peace (13:11–13)

That's all I have to say. Now back to the formal matters we always use to close a letter. We want to bless you with God's blessings. We want you to rejoice in all God is doing among you. We want you to mature into God's perfect way. Live in peace and unity with one another and with God. Know God's loving presence. Maintain the fellowship by continuing to greet each member with the customary kiss on each cheek. Receive greetings from God's people who are with me.

■ TRUTHS TO LIVE BY

Discipline is necessary for the church to grow. Preachers don't like to do it any more than Paul did, but a church must face up to its sins as a body and as individuals. Sin must be cleared from the church so God's power can work in and through it.

Discipline reveals Christ in your life. Each member must regularly take a spiritual self-examination and let Christ show any imperfections and sins. Then comes time to submit to Christ's discipline to purge from your life anything that prevents you from being what Christ wants. Then you will truly experience Christ in you, and the world will see Christ through you.

Discipline brings church unity in God's love, peace, and truth. A church that practices and endures discipline finds itself united in Christ's love, experiencing God's wholeness and peace in life, and teaching God's truth.

■ A VERSE TO REMEMBER

Examine yourselves, whether ye be in the faith; prove your own selves. Know ye not your own selves, how that Jesus Christ is in you, except ye be reprobates?—2 Corinthians 13:5

■ DAILY BIBLE READINGS

May 22 — Paul Defends His Ministry. 2 Cor. 10:1–11
May 23 — If You Boast, Boast in the Lord. 2 Cor. 10:12–18
May 24 — Paul and the False Apostles. 2 Cor. 11:1–15
May 25 — Paul's Sufferings as an Apostle. 2 Cor. 11:16–29
May 26 — Paul's Visions and Revelations. 2 Cor. 12:1–10
May 27 — Paul's Concern for the Corinthian Christians. 2 Cor. 12:11–21
May 28 — Live in Faith: Christ Is in You. 2 Cor. 13:1–13

Living Is Christ

Basic Passage: Philippians 1:12–26

In prison for preaching. How do you respond? Paul had been proven innocent before Roman judges in Palestine but had appealed to Rome to escape Jewish sabotage. In Rome, chained to a prison guard, he told people about Christ and wrote to the churches he loved. The next thirteen weeks we read letters from prison to churches needing a prisoner's word of hope. Here Paul helps the churches and helps us see the basics of Christian living.

THE BIBLE LESSON

Philippians 1

12 But I would ye should understand, brethren, that the things which happened unto me have fallen out rather unto the furtherance of the gospel;

13 So that my bonds in Christ are manifest in all the palace, and in all other places;

14 And many of the brethren in the Lord, waxing confident by my bonds, are much more bold to speak the word without fear.

15 Some indeed preach Christ even of envy and strife; and some also of good will:

16 The one preach Christ of contention, not sincerely, supposing to add affliction to my bonds:

17 But the other of love, knowing that I am set for the defence of the gospel.

18 What then? notwithstanding, every way, whether in pretense, or in truth, Christ is preached; and I therein do rejoice, yea, and will rejoice.

19 For I know that this shall turn to my salvation through your prayer, and the supply of the Spirit of Jesus Christ,

20 According to my earnest expectation and my hope, that in nothing I shall be ashamed, but that with all boldness, as

*always, so now also Christ shall be magnified in my body,
whether it be by life, or by death.*

21 For to me to live is Christ, and to die is gain.

*22 But if I live in the flesh, this is the fruit of my labour: yet
what I shall choose I wot not.*

*23 For I am in a strait betwixt two, having a desire to
depart, and to be with Christ; which is far better:*

*24 Nevertheless to abide in the flesh is more needful for
you.*

*25 And having this confidence, I know that I shall abide
and continue with you all for your furtherance and joy of
faith;*

*26 That your rejoicing may be more abundant in Jesus
Christ for me by my coming to you again.*

■ THE LESSON EXPLAINED

In Prison for Christ (1:12–18)

Philippians is Paul's ode of joy to a church he enjoyed.
The church was not overjoyed to find Paul in jail. They worried about him. Paul reassured them they had nothing to
worry about. He was in jail for a purpose, to serve Christ.
Even people throughout the palace of the Roman emperor
became familiar with the gospel because Paul did time in a
Roman prison. Other Christians, seeing Paul's example,
gained courage and spoke out for Christ more strongly than
they ever had before. Of course, some saw how popular and
famous Paul was becoming and tried to imitate him so they
could have his fame. Such preaching from envy still led
people to Christ, so Paul rejoiced. Whatever the motive of
preaching, Paul encouraged people to keep preaching so
others would keep hearing about Christ. Rejoice!

Living Is Christ; Dying Is Profit (1:19–24)

Paul was sure God was with him, even in prison, and
would bring the kind of deliverance Paul needed. The
church's prayers and the Spirit's presence were all the

resources Paul needed. Paul wanted simply to maintain his witness so he would not be ashamed of himself. As long as he lived, he worked to bring glory to Christ. Even in death he expected to have people honor and glorify Christ. Living meant showing other people Christ. Dying meant being with Christ. Which was better? For the church, his living and preaching was better. For him personally, being with Christ was better. The choice was difficult: continue bearing fruit for Christ or being with Christ? Meet the church's needs or his desires?

Dedicated to Your Growth and Joy (1:25,26)

God gave Paul confidence that he would not die just yet. He would continue to help the church. Then the church would mature in faith and grow in joy. He even expected to visit Philippi again and see the great joy that would bring to the church—joy not for who Paul was or for what Paul did, but joy for what Jesus did in delivering Paul and bringing him to them.

■ TRUTHS TO LIVE BY

Preaching Christ is our priority. Where we are, the conditions we face, the troubles that beset us . . . nothing matters. Our lifestyle should not change. Preaching to others about Jesus should be our first and foremost goal in life.

Death is best. Life on earth continually brings problems, frustrations, pains, heartaches. Death brings separation only for the moment but salvation for eternity. Surely for each believer in Christ, the state after death is better than the state of life on earth.

Life is given to help others. Life on earth has one purpose: Bring God's joy to others, first by letting them hear and respond to the gospel of salvation, and second by leading them to grow in Christ.

■ A VERSE TO REMEMBER

For to me to live is Christ, and to die is gain.
—*Philippians 1:21*

■ DAILY BIBLE READINGS

May 29 — Paul's Prayer for the Philippians. Phil. 1:1–11
May 30 — Prison Bars Cannot Imprison the Gospel.
　　　　　Phil. 1:12–18a
May 31 — Paul Exalts Christ in Life or Death.
　　　　　Phil. 1:18b–26
June 1 — Stand Firm in Suffering. Phil. 1:27–30
June 2 — We Have a Living Hope in Christ. 1 Pet. 1:3–9
June 3 — A Call to Holy Living. 1 Pet. 1:17–25
June 4 — Living Stones of the Living Stone. 1 Pet. 2:1–10

Having the Mind of Christ

Basic Passage: Philippians 2:1–13

Samson continues on our mind as we prepare to go to Kenya next week. Samson is preparing all the details for our arrival. Samson will have all the churches ready to greet us. Samson will let any church or pastor that has not done its part know what must be done now. Samson will have a goal for us to reach as we witness to individuals about Christ and help start new churches in Kenya. We fear what would happen to us should Samson not be able to be our guide in Kenya. Why is Samson so valuable? He has Christ's mind in him guiding each decision he makes and each action he takes. He sees God at work and gets involved immediately, even though work like ours may be hundreds of miles away from his home. Oh, to have in our country more people like that wonderful Kenyan, people propelled by the mind of Christ.

■ THE BIBLE LESSON

Philippians 2

1 If there be therefore any consolation in Christ, if any comfort of love, if any fellowship of the Spirit, if any bowels and mercies,

2 Fulfill ye my joy, that ye be likeminded, having the same love, being of one accord, of one mind.

3 Let nothing be done through strife or vainglory; but in lowliness of mind let each esteem other better than themselves.

4 Look not every man on his own things, but every man also on the things of others.

5 Let this mind be in you, which was also in Christ Jesus:

6 Who, being in the form of God, thought it not robbery to be equal with God:

7 But made himself of no reputation, and took upon him the form of a servant, and was made in the likeness of men:

8 And being found in fashion as a man, he humbled himself, and became obedient unto death, even the death of the cross.

9 Wherefore God also hath highly exalted him, and given him a name which is above every name:

10 That at the name of Jesus every knee should bow, of things in heaven, and things in earth, and things under the earth;

11 And that every tongue should confess that Jesus Christ is Lord, to the glory of God the Father.

12 Wherefore, my beloved, as ye have always obeyed, not as in my presence only, but now much more in my absence, work out your own salvation with fear and trembling.

13 For it is God which worketh in you both to will and to do of his good pleasure.

■ THE LESSON EXPLAINED

Concentrate on Others (2:1–4)

Are you a Christian believer? Do you experience comfort from Christ in time of hurt and sorrow? Do you find His love consoles you when all others desert you? Does His Spirit provide the friendship and fellowship you need when people are nowhere to be seen? Do you find that sense of being loved and cared for from Christ? Then listen up. Some things for you to do!

Make my joy bubble over the top by agreeing with one another, loving one another, having the same attitudes, and working toward the same purpose as Christ did. Don't try to outdo one another or get the best of one another. Don't fight other believers. Take Christ's outlook on life, that of humility. View other people and their needs as more important than you and your desires. Quit protecting what you have and what you are interested in. Keep a protective eye on the other believers' interests.

Imitate Christ's Humility (2:5–11)

How can we be that good? Imitate Christ. Let His attitude be our attitude. Let Christ's mind dominate our mind. Think about Him. He is God and could have justifiably said He was equal with God: "I and the Father are one." Still, He did not insist on maintaining such a high status. He gave away his reputation and power as God to come to earth as a tiny human baby. He did not lord it over people here, but became their servant, washing their feet. Even though He was a human being, He still went the extra mile. He became the most despised of people, a criminal sentenced to capital punishment on the cruel cross.

Why? That was the Father's plan. He obeyed it. What happened then? God exalted the crucified One. God raised Him from the dead. God gave Him a reputation greater than any person who ever lived. One day everyone who has ever lived will recognize the position Christ occupies. They will fall on their faces, confess who He is, and worship Him. God's plan will be accomplished. He will get all the glory for what He did through Jesus' death. Be like Jesus.

Let God Work His Will in You (2:12,13)

You have always done what I asked and what God expected. Keep on that course even if I cannot be with you. Christ saved you. In humble awe and fear, live the life of salvation. Be the kind of person Christ was. See where God is at work in your world. Join Him in that work. Let Him work in you and through you. You will see God accomplishing what He enjoys doing. You will see God's eternal plan of salvation coming to pass on earth through you as it is now in heaven. The humble mind of Christ in you will let you do this.

■   TRUTHS TO LIVE BY

Humility unites in loving and in helping others. By being humble as Christ was humble, you unite the people of God in service to one another and to the world. You omit selfishness and self-righteousness from the church's playbook, and let them play under Christ's rules, the rules of love and servanthood.

Humility lives as Christ lived. Humility is not a state you achieve. It is a life you let Christ live in you. Christ is the only humble one. The rest of us are too dominated by the self-centered, God-doubting life of Adam. Let Christ live in you. His mind will make you humble.

Humility lets God work through you. The human mind seeks self-importance and personal achievement. Christ's mind seeks to accomplish God's purposes and do His work. Surrender to Christ gives you the humble attitude God can use to work through you toward His saving goal for all humanity and the world.

■ A VERSE TO REMEMBER

Let this mind be in you, which was also in Christ Jesus.—Philippians 2:5

■ DAILY BIBLE READINGS

June 5 — Imitate Christ's Humility in Your Lives.
Phil. 2:1–11
June 6 — Rejoice in One Another's Faithfulness.
Phil. 2:12–18
June 7 — Timothy, a Faithful Servant of Christ.
Phil. 2:19–24
June 8 — Welcome Epaphroditus in Christ. Phil. 2:25–30
June 9 — Repay Evil with a Blessing. 1 Pet. 3:8–12
June 10— Suffering for Doing Right. 1 Pet. 3:13–22
June 11— You Are Participants in God's Nature.
2 Pet. 1:1–11

Pressing on in Christ

Basic Passage: Philippians 3:7–21

At ten years of age I began working in my father's book-keeping office. He quickly introduced me to the ledger, a big book with many columns recording the financial operations of the grocery chain. I not only had to learn to copy the exact figures; I had to know which column to put each figure in. Paul compared life to a bookkeeping system. He showed us which columns to put ourselves in.

■ THE BIBLE LESSON

Philippians 3

7 But what things were gain to me, those I counted loss for Christ.

8 Yea doubtless, and I count all things but loss for the excellency of the knowledge of Christ Jesus my Lord: for whom I have suffered the loss of all things, and do count them but dung, that I may win Christ,

9 And be found in him, not having mine own righteousness, which is of the law, but that which is through the faith of Christ, the righteousness which is of God by faith:

10 That I may know him, and the power of his resurrection, and the fellowship of his sufferings, being made conformable unto his death;

11 If by any means I might attain unto the resurrection of the dead.

12 Not as though I had already attained, either were already perfect: but I follow after, if that I may apprehend that for which also I am apprehended of Christ Jesus.

13 Brethren, I count not myself to have apprehended: but this one thing I do, forgetting those things which are behind, and reaching forth unto those things which are before,

14 I press toward the mark for the prize of the high calling of God in Christ Jesus.

15 Let us therefore, as many as be perfect, be thus minded: and if in any thing ye be otherwise minded, God shall reveal even this unto you.

16 Nevertheless, whereto we have already attained, let us walk by the same rule, let us mind the same thing.

17 Brethren, be followers together of me, and mark them which walk so as ye have us for an ensample.

18 (For many walk, of whom I have told you often, and now tell you even weeping, that they are the enemies of the cross of Christ:

19 Whose end is destruction, whose God is their belly, and whose glory is in their shame, who mind earthly things.)

20 For our conversation is in heaven; from whence also we look for the Saviour, the Lord Jesus Christ:

21 Who shall change our vile body, that it may be fashioned like unto his glorious body, according to the working whereby he is able even to subdue all things unto himself.

■ THE LESSON EXPLAINED

All in the Loss Column (3:7–9)

Learn, Paul pleads, from my experience. I got as high in the Jewish religious system as I could go. Everyone knew me. Everyone admired me. Life was all in the plus column, all under profits. Then I met Jesus on the Damascus road. He taught me a whole new bookkeeping system. Everything I had put in the profits column I transferred to the loss column. I had been counting the wrong things as profit. My business was in a mess. You might say I lost everything: position, profits, profile, popularity. That matters nothing. I have thrown it all on the garbage pile. I will do it all over again if I gain Christ. Knowing Him is all that matters. I thought I was righteous and accepted by God because I obeyed the Jewish law. That was all hogwash. I am accepted as righteous by God only when I have faith in Christ. Faith is all that can be entered in the profits column.

Resurrection in the Profit Column (3:10–14)

Faith in Christ brings what He can give and no one else can—resurrection and a personal relationship with Jesus. This relationship means I carry my cross as He carried His. I will suffer and die because I believe in Him. No matter! He will raise my dead body from the grave. I want to grab hold of Christ and His resurrection. Have not quite made it yet. Must learn from Him and obey Him, but He has grabbed hold of me and that is all that matters. Yes, I had everything a Jew could want. I threw it all away, put it all in the loss column gladly. I forgot about it all. I have one thing in view. God has called me to be like Jesus and to share in His death and His resurrection. I want to be what God is calling me to be. Nothing else!

Obedience in the Operations Column (3:15–21)

If you are mature in Christ, then you want to know how to operate for Him. You know operation expense is a major part of business, and you want to know the operation expenses in following Christ. You are to have the same goal I do: fulfilling God's calling for you. To do this, you have to mature and become complete in Christ. If you do not have this goal and operate life to accomplish God's calling, then God will let you know about it. Need an example here on earth to follow? Look at me. I am doing the best I know how. Imitate me as I imitate Christ.

Beware, you have a lot of others who would be your example, but they are concerned only with things of this world, with material profit and loss. I hate to say it. It makes me cry, but these would-be examples are really enemies of the cross. They do not seek God's calling and do not take up the cross to die for Christ. They are citizens of earth. We are citizens of heaven. One day Jesus, our Savior, is coming back down from heaven to get us. Then we will know the resurrection and have all the profits we need. He will give us the resurrection body, and we will live forever with Him in heaven. Then He will rule everything always.

■ TRUTHS TO LIVE BY

Recognize your profits are losses for Christ. You may have a lot of worldly accomplishments and marvelous bank accounts. Trade in your resumé and your possessions. Take them out of the profit column. One thing belongs there: God's calling for you in Christ.

Set resurrection as your life's goal. Every business has a mission. For most it is making money. Christ has changed our mission. Our mission is to follow Him in faith until He raises us from the dead as God raised Him.

Obey until resurrection comes. Until resurrection comes, life with Christ is the goal. Daily life with Jesus is a life of daily obedience, doing what Jesus says, going where He leads, and being the kind of humble person Jesus is.

■ A VERSE TO REMEMBER

I press toward the mark for the prize of the high calling of God in Christ Jesus.—Philippians 3:14

■ DAILY BIBLE READINGS

June 12— Don't Be Led Astray. Phil. 3:1–6
June 13— The Ultimate Richness: Knowing Jesus Christ. Phil. 3:7–11
June 14— Press on Toward the Goal. Phil. 3:12–16
June 15— Our Citizenship in Heaven. Phil. 3:17–4:1
June 16— Encourage One Another in Christ Jesus. Heb. 10:19–25
June 17— Hold Fast Your Confidence in Christ. Heb. 10:26–39
June 18— Live a Disciplined Christian Life. Heb. 12:1–13

Rejoicing in Christ

Basic Passage: Philippians 4:4–18

I was so mad last night. The world fell in around me. I created a scenario in my mind of total chaos. No more reason to live. Death almost seemed inviting. Then I began praying. It did not settle the issue, but I gained the peace to sleep. This morning as I drove to work, I shut off the radio and began praying again. Suddenly, deep peace and joy settled in my heart. This was much more than the joy of hearing, "It's a boy!" or "Surprise, Grandma's here!" This was joy that let me walk through the same world that wrecked my soul last night with the confidence of God's presence and life's worth and meaning. That's deep joy, God's gift of joy.

▮ THE BIBLE LESSON

Philippians 4

4 Rejoice in the Lord alway: and again I say, Rejoice.

5 Let your moderation be known unto all men. The Lord is at hand.

6 Be careful for nothing; but in every thing by prayer and supplication with thanksgiving let your requests be made known unto God.

7 And the peace of God, which passeth all understanding, shall keep your hearts and minds through Christ Jesus.

8 Finally, brethren, whatsoever things are true, whatsoever things are honest, whatsoever things are just, whatsoever things are pure, whatsoever things are lovely, whatsoever things are of good report; if there be any virtue, and if there be any praise, think on these things.

9 Those things, which ye have both learned, and received, and heard, and seen in me, do: and the God of peace shall be with you.

10 But I rejoiced in the Lord greatly, that now at the last your care of me hath flourished again; wherein ye were also careful, but ye lacked opportunity.

11 Not that I speak in respect of want: for I have learned, in whatsoever state I am, therewith to be content.

12 I know both how to be abased, and I know how to abound: every where and in all things I am instructed both to be full and to be hungry, both to abound and to suffer need.

13 I can do all things through Christ which strengtheneth me.

14 Notwithstanding ye have well done, that ye did communicate with my affliction.

15 Now ye Philippians know also, that in the beginning of the gospel, when I departed from Macedonia, no church communicated with me as concerning giving and receiving, but ye only.

16 For even in Thessalonica ye sent once and again unto my necessity.

17 Not because I desire a gift: but I desire fruit that may abound to your account.

18 But I have all, and abound: I am full, having received of Epaphroditus the things which were sent from you, an odour of a sweet smell, a sacrifice acceptable, well pleasing to God.

■ THE LESSON EXPLAINED

Rejoice and Pray (4:4–7)

Chapter four is Paul's course in practical theology for the church at Philippi. They are "my brothers, you whom I love and long for, my joy and crown" (v. 1). Yet he has to call for unity (vv. 2, 3). How do you do this? You rejoice in God all the time, not giving yourself time to think envious thoughts about others and not allowing negative emotions to enter your life. Concentration on God's joy makes you gentle, compassionate, able to moderate your problems with other people, understanding their viewpoint rather than standing on yours. Most of all, you pray, thanking God for His goodness and gifts, giving all worries over to Him, and telling Him the deepest longings of your heart.

Rejoice and Behave (4:8, 9)

Unity with fellow believers comes from rejoicing in God, praying to God, and behaving before God. Behaving comes not from listing rules and obeying them. Behaving comes from thinking about good things, virtuous things, rather than thinking about gripes you have against other people. Truth eliminates gossip. Honesty eliminates making up tales. Justice prevents prejudice and manipulation. Purity prevents wrongdoing. Loveliness erases ugly actions. Good report stops you from ruining a reputation. Virtue maintains your identity as a Christian, and praise forms your attitude to God and others. Such thoughts put into action in imitation of a mentor like Paul lead God to provide inner peace which cannot be interrupted to create outer chaos.

Rejoice and Care (4:10–18)

Passing from mild rebuke, Paul explains his joy. The Philippians sent help while he was in prison, demonstrating in action their love and care for him. He knows this was the first opportunity they had to do so, and he rejoices. Such care cements relationships more than it provides for urgent needs. Paul had learned in his imprisonments and persecutions to get by on a lot less than most people considered the bare minimum. How? By leaning on Christ's strength and depending on His provision. The gift of care becomes dearer when it becomes a habit of life as it had for the Philippians with Paul. This showed the fruit of the gospel growing in their lives. It functioned as a sacrificial offering, pleasing God. Anything that pleased God pleased Paul, especially the caring gift Epaphroditus brought to the Roman prison from Philippi. So Paul and the Philippians could rest assured in their mutual caring that God would provide all either needed. So glory be to God!

■ TRUTHS TO LIVE BY

Joy comes through personal relationship with Jesus. Joy never exists apart from Jesus. He is the Fountain of Joy. Faith in Him lived out in trust and love brings His deep joy.

Joy comes through obedient living. Joy comes from a heart committed to virtuous thoughts and loving acts. A life of sin never produces joy. A life of pure obedience always does.

Joy comes through caring for and helping others. Joy deserts the self-centered life. Joy invades and occupies the life dedicated to the needs and hopes of others.

■ A VERSE TO REMEMBER

Rejoice in the Lord alway: and again I say, Rejoice.
—Philippians 4:4

■ DAILY BIBLE READINGS

June 19 — Rejoice, and Be Gentle with One Another.
Phil. 4:2–7
June 20 — Keep on Keeping on in Christ. Phil. 4:8–14
June 21 — Paul's Thanks for the Philippian Church.
Phil. 4:15–23
June 22 — Life among the Early Believers. Acts 2:43–47
June 23 — Paul's Thanks for the Thessalonian Church.
1 Thess. 1:1–10
June 24 — Lives Pleasing to God. 1 Thess. 4:1–12
June 25 — Faithfulness Brings Great Joy. 3 John 1–8

Called to Spiritual Blessings in Christ

Basic Passage: Ephesians 1:1–14

Walking the roads and paths of Kenya, I discovered the meaning of blessing. As Kenyan pastors and the "church mother" led me from house to house, I could see their mounting excitement come from watching people in their neighborhood come to know Jesus as Savior. I watched the eyes of those who prayed to accept Christ and to have their sins forgiven. Joy and hope and praise sparkled in the eyes of people whose lips could not say a word I understood. Spiritual blessings abounded in these lives, those taking the gospel and those receiving it.

■ THE BIBLE LESSON

Ephesians 1

1 Paul, an apostle of Jesus Christ by the will of God, to the saints which are at Ephesus, and to the faithful in Christ Jesus:

2 Grace be to you, and peace, from God our Father, and from the Lord Jesus Christ.

3 Blessed be the God and Father of our Lord Jesus Christ, who hath blessed us with all spiritual blessings in heavenly places in Christ:

4 According as he hath chosen us in him before the foundation of the world, that we should be holy and without blame before him in love:

5 Having predestinated us unto the adoption of children by Jesus Christ to himself, according to the good pleasure of his will,

6 To the praise of the glory of his grace, wherein he hath made us accepted in the beloved.

7 In whom we have redemption through his blood, the for-giveness of sins, according to the riches of his grace;

8 Wherein he hath abounded toward us in all wisdom and prudence;

9 Having made known unto us the mystery of his will, according to his good pleasure which he hath purposed in himself:

10 That in the dispensation of the fullness of times he might gather together in one all things in Christ, both which are in heaven, and which are on earth; even in him:

11 In whom also we have obtained an inheritance, being predestinated according to the purpose of him who worketh all things after the counsel of his own will:

12 That we should be to the praise of his glory, who first trusted in Christ.

13 In whom ye also trusted, after that ye heard the word of truth, the gospel of your salvation: in whom also after that ye believed, ye were sealed with that holy Spirit of promise,

14 Which is the earnest of our inheritance until the redemption of the purchased possession, unto the praise of his glory.

■ THE LESSON EXPLAINED

All Spiritual Blessings (1:1-3)

Using the normal introductory formulas of a Greek letter, Paul addresses God's saints, those set apart to be His holy representatives on earth—that is, every church member. Such are faithful to God's will in Christ. Thus, Paul can bless them with God's peace and grace. At the same time he blesses or praises God for sending every spiritual blessing the people could possibly need. Such blessings have their home in the heavens, not on earth. Their source is God and Him alone. These are spiritual blessings, blessings from the Holy Spirit. They provide believers with heaven's resources to face life's circumstances. We can receive such blessings because we are in Christ. We have trusted our lives to Him in faith.

Blessing of Redemption (1:4–7)

Divine blessing has nothing to do with human earning power. God decided to make this available long before He created humans, even before He created the earth. He decided to bless us so we could be holy and pure as He is, and so we could love Him and love one another, making love our defining characteristic as it is His (1 John 4:8). God planned the fact of redemption and the way of redemption. Jesus Christ, His only Son, would provide redemption by dying on the cross so He could adopt us as His children, thus satisfying Himself completely.

We see this as a gift of grace—God accepting us as sons through His beloved Son when we did not deserve it. So we praise God for His grace. Salvation means God forgave us, covered our sins with His blood.

Blessing of Revelation (1:8–10)

God in His great wisdom and understanding showered His grace on us, letting us know the mystery of His eternal plan of salvation, a plan made possible because He was lovingly disposed toward us and planned to save us in Christ. The plan will be complete when the end of time comes and God gathers His full church, all those who believe in Christ, to Himself—citizens of heaven and earth who believe in Him.

Blessing of Trust in Christ (1:11–14)

God's wonderful grace plan includes me. I am His heir because He planned it all out before the world began. What He plans, He has the power and will to accomplish. He said if I trusted Christ, I would be saved. I trusted. I am saved. God's Holy Spirit sealed me in order to deliver me to Him in heaven in that day. That seal is the down payment of my salvation, letting me know for sure I am His and am safely saved. Praise God. To Him be the glory.

■ TRUTHS TO LIVE BY

You are blessed to be God's children. Salvation is not something to take for granted. In eternity God planned it. In time He created it through Christ's death. In grace He included me. I have blessing from the Spirit given by God because I believe in Christ.

You are blessed to know His will. God did not keep salvation a secret that I had to search to know. He called His people to preach His gospel so I would know how to be saved. What a blessing to know His way of salvation.

You are blessed to have an eternal inheritance. Salvation is not just for the moment or just for a lifetime. Trust in Christ now means life with Christ forever. Praise God.

■ A VERSE TO REMEMBER

Blessed be the God and Father of our Lord Jesus Christ, who hath blessed us with all spiritual blessings in heavenly places in Christ.—Ephesians 1:3

■ DAILY BIBLE READINGS

June 26— God Has Blessed Us in Christ. Eph. 1:1–6
June 27— God's Grace Lavished on Us in Christ.
              Eph. 1:7–14
June 28— Paul's Prayer for the Ephesian Christians.
              Eph. 1:15–23
June 29— Called to Belong to Jesus Christ. Rom. 1:1–7
June 30— The Gospel: God's Power for Salvation.
              Rom. 1:8–17
July 1   — Bear the Fruit of the Spirit. Gal. 5:16–26
July 2   — Bear One Another's Burdens. Gal. 6:1–10

Called to Oneness in Christ

Basic Passage: Ephesians 2:8–22

Facing Polish Christians on the eastern border as they
are waiting for the Russian tanks visible in the trees to
attack their homes. Praying in a Yugoslavian hotel, neither
able to understand the language of the other but equally
unable to miss the Spirit in the other. Preaching the ordina-
tion sermon of a young black pastor, knowing some of my
deacons across the valley and up the hill might have shot-
guns waiting, should the young man enter our church. Witnessing through Kenyan interpreters into Swahili and
Tesso as hundreds of men and women accept Christ as Savior. Teaching to students from forty different countries at
the same time. Watching Arabs and Jews worship Christ
together in a small church. Yes, God has let me see a glimmer of the unity He wants in His church. May our day see
that unity overcome all prejudice and hate and language
and cultural barriers so we are truly one in Christ.

■ THE BIBLE LESSON

Ephesians 2

*8 For by grace are ye saved through faith; and that not of
yourselves: it is the gift of God:*

9 Not of works, lest any man should boast.

*10 For we are his workmanship, created in Christ Jesus
unto good works, which God hath before ordained that we
should walk in them.*

*11 Wherefore remember, that ye being in time past Gen-
tiles in the flesh, who are called Uncircumcision by that
which is called the Circumcision in the flesh made by hands;*

*12 That at that time ye were without Christ, being aliens
from the commonwealth of Israel, and strangers from the cov-
enants of promise, having no hope, and without God in the
world:*

13 But now in Christ Jesus ye who sometimes were far off are made nigh by the blood of Christ.

14 For he is our peace, who hath made both one, and hath broken down the middle wall of partition between us;

15 Having abolished in his flesh the enmity, even the law of commandments contained in ordinances; for to make in himself of twain one new man, so making peace;

16 And that he might reconcile both unto God in one body by the cross, having slain the enmity thereby:

17 And came and preached peace to you which were afar off, and to them that were nigh.

18 For through him we both have access by one Spirit unto the Father.

19 Now therefore ye are no more strangers and foreigners, but fellowcitizens with the saints, and of the household of God;

20 And are built upon the foundation of the apostles and prophets, Jesus Christ himself being the chief corner stone;

21 In whom all the building fitly framed together groweth unto an holy temple in the Lord:

22 In whom ye also are builded together for an habitation of God through the Spirit.

■ THE LESSON EXPLAINED

Saved by Grace for Works (2:8–10)

Do you know the ABCs of Christianity? Learn them again. Salvation comes as you trust Jesus, not as you live a life that somehow earns salvation. You can never get on the plus side of the ledger with God. You are always in debt to Him. He died for you. He gave you salvation. You never have reason to brag. He did it all. God created us. He re-created us sinners through the blood of Christ. He wants us to obey Him and help other people. Why? To earn salvation? No! You can never do enough. To express our gratitude and trust in Him who knows what is best for us? Of course. Trust and obey.

Saved from Pagan Worship (2:11–17)

How do I know I do not deserve salvation? I know where I came from, a life dedicated to pagan, sinful practices, not devoted to God. I came from a people who originally had no knowledge of the true God, because they were not part of His people, the Jews. I had no promise from God and had made no promise to God. Christ came. Christ died. Jews preached His gospel. My people heard it. They believed. They taught me. I believed. I am saved. Because of what I did? No! Because Christ died. Now both Jews and non-Jews can be saved. Christ's death destroyed all barriers between them. His death cut down the temple veil in which Jewish rites brought atonement to Jews only. He destroyed the Jewish system of righteousness by obedience to law. He made peace between Jews and non-Jews. We are all one people in Him.

Saved to Know the Father (2:18–22)

Salvation at its most basic is a relationship in which you know God personally. This is possible because God puts His Spirit in your heart. He joins us to His church with equal rights with every other member. Our faith goes back to the faith of the twelve apostles who first believed and preached the gospel. Theirs rests on the Old Testament prophets, who pointed the way to Jesus. All find unity in Jesus, who built us all together into one body. Thus, we as former Jews or former non-Jews are one holy temple, exemplifying Christ to the world. That means God lives in us. The world sees God as they see us. God works as His Spirit works through us.

■ TRUTHS TO LIVE BY

You do not deserve salvation. You are a sinner. You deserve God's condemnation. He does not want to condemn. He is love and wants to save. Will you trust Him for salvation? or yourself?

You are saved by God's grace in Christ. Salvation is possible because God in eternity planned to send Jesus to die on the cross for you. God did this because He loves you. He gave the gift of His Son, the most precious possible gift. Will you take the gift from God?

You are called to be God's holy house. Having believed, you have a responsibility and opportunity to live holy lives that will lead others to Christ.

■ A VERSE TO REMEMBER

Now therefore ye are no more strangers and foreigners, but fellowcitizens with the saints, and of the household of God.—Ephesians 2:19

■ DAILY BIBLE READINGS

July 3 — Saved and Made Alive by Grace. Eph. 2:1–10
July 4 — One Body in Jesus Christ. Eph. 2:11–16
July 5 — God Dwells in You. Eph. 2:17–22
July 6 — Jesus Commits Disciples to God's Care. John 17:1–6
July 7 — Jesus Prays for the Disciples' Protection. John 17:7–13
July 8 — Jesus Prays for the Disciples' Unity. John 17:14–21
July 9 — May God's Love Be in Christ's Disciples. John 17:22–26

Called to Use Your Spiritual Gifts

Basic Passage: Ephesians 4:1–16

Retired from work, but full time on God's employment list. She takes three or so mission trips each year, spending what money she has for gifts to take to the people she works with on the mission field and people she witnesses to. And what a witness. Looking at this grandmother, one might question what she could do in the wilds of Kenya. Is it not dangerous to her health and to the welfare of the others in the group to risk taking her with us? Then watch her at work. See the kids gather round to listen to her. See her love for every person she meets, a love that flows from Christ's love for her. Listen to the reports each evening. She can always report that she has led as many people to Christ as anyone else. She has found her spiritual gift—talking to people. She uses it to tell them about the Lord.

▮ THE BIBLE LESSON

Ephesians 4

1 I therefore, the prisoner of the Lord, beseech you that ye walk worthy of the vocation wherewith ye are called,

2 With all lowliness and meekness, with longsuffering, forbearing one another in love;

3 Endeavoring to keep the unity of the Spirit in the bond of peace.

4 There is one body, and one Spirit, even as ye are called in one hope of your calling;

5 One Lord, one faith, one baptism,

6 One God and Father of all, who is above all, and through all, and in you all.

7 But unto every one of us is given grace according to the measure of the gift of Christ.

8 Wherefore he saith, When he ascended up on high, he led captivity captive, and gave gifts unto men.

9 (Now that he ascended, what is it but that he also descended first into the lower parts of the earth?

10 He that descended is the same also that ascended up far above all heavens, that he might fill all things.)

11 And he gave some, apostles; and some, prophets; and some, evangelists; and some, pastors and teachers;

12 For the perfecting of the saints, for the work of the ministry, for the edifying of the body of Christ:

13 Till we all come in the unity of the faith, and of the knowledge of the Son of God, unto a perfect man, unto the measure of the stature of the fulness of Christ:

14 That we henceforth be no more children, tossed to and fro, and carried about with every wind of doctrine, by the sleight of men, and cunning craftiness, whereby they lie in wait to deceive;

15 But speaking the truth in love, may grow up into him in all things, which is the head, even Christ:

16 From whom the whole body fitly joined together and compacted by that which every joint supplieth, according to the effectual working in the measure of every part, maketh increase of the body unto the edifying of itself in love.

◼ THE LESSON EXPLAINED

The Way that is Worthy (4:1–3)

Every life needs a road map. Paul drew one for every believer. Following the map led him to prison; still, he recommended this way for everyone. His worthy way led you to hold up the honor of Christ and to show the world how He has called you to His service. To walk the path requires a special kind of person, one who is willing to take the low road, not the high one. This means putting others before yourself and not trying to make a name for yourself. It means accepting the scorn of the world to achieve the purposes of Christ. It means overlooking the mistakes and attitudes of others, loving them into Christ's way. It means seeking peace and unity within the church, no matter what it costs you or what others think of you. Why? The Spirit indwells and leads you in the worthy way.

The Way of Oneness (4:4–6)

What's the alternative route? Is there not a detour where I can save some of my own desires and reputation and still be on Christ's way? NO! exclaims Paul, as he lists the ones of Christ's one way. The church is one and must stay on one way together. The Spirit is one and leads only in one way. Your calling gives you one hope to reach one destination. You have one Lord, Jesus. You have one faith; trust in Him. You were baptized one time, in the name of the Trinity. You have one sovereign God who controls all and lives in each church member. The church is one on one way. Don't seek a detour.

The Way of Gifts (4:7–12)

Do these ones of the faith mean we all have to be alike, clones of each other? You know better. Christ gave each of us gifts to use in His church. Using your gifts makes you distinctive, a unique part of His body, the church. Remember Psalm 68:18 told us Christ would ascend, the victor over all powers and demonic forces, and that He would give gifts to people. Of course, before He could ascend to heaven, He had to descend to earth.

It is the incarnate Christ who gives you gifts. You have received His spiritual gifts. Each of these assists the church in His ministry: the apostles to preserve the tradition about Jesus and do missionary work; prophets to interpret God's Word and God's will to the church; evangelists to lead people to accept Christ; pastors and teachers to lead the church in the way of Christ. All these gifts used together serve one purpose: they enhance the Christian life of every church member, seeking to bring each to maturity so that the church may grow and be the body of Christ.

The Way of Growth (4:13–16)

What is church growth? It is all believers together achieving the place in Christian faith that God has gifted them to reach. It is working together as one body joined by the same faith in Christ to have a personal relationship with God's Son, being the obedient, loving person day by day that God expects, and eventually becoming just like Christ. Such people do not fall for the tricks and fancy speech of false teachers. They know Christ too well personally. They stay with the church, not with the new, fancy-talking, self-seeking teachers. Christ's people learn to talk to one another in love so the church truly represents the loving Christ to the world. Then the body of Christ is truly one, using the gifts and calling of each of its members to achieve Christ's purposes.

■ TRUTHS TO LIVE BY

Humility and love mark God's worthy path. Spiritual gifts lead a person to amazement in the grace of Christ and to humility in the use of spiritual gifts for the good of the church. Gifts lead us to love the church and its head, not ourselves and our gifts.

Gifts build up the church, not the individual. Spiritual gifts have one purpose, to mature the church so it can accomplish Christ's purposes and truly represent Him. Gifts never furnish a Christian reason for pride, bragging, or thinking oneself better than another. Gifts do not measure personal maturity, but help the church as a body to mature.

Gifts grow the body in love to be like Christ. Gifts, rightly used, lead each member to respect and admire every other member. Gifts join together in common cause to grow the church in maturity and numbers. Gifts lead to love, not envy; to cooperation, not individual effort.

▪ A VERSE TO REMEMBER

But unto every one of us is given grace according to the measure of the gift of Christ.—Ephesians 4:7

▪ DAILY BIBLE READINGS

Called to Responsible Living

Basic Passage: Ephesians 5:1–5, 21–29; 6:1–4

Our mission to Kenya last summer caused some problems for the Kenyan believers. Our naive attempt to help the churches encouraged us to take gifts to give the pastors, and senior mothers, and translators, and evangelists who helped us through the two weeks of witnessing. When we got back, we found we had stirred some jealousy in the church as some people wanted the small gifts others had received. Fortunately, Kenya has Samson. This wonderful Christian leader soon set the Kenyans straight. They had to live responsibly for God, not in jealousy toward one another.

■ THE BIBLE LESSON

Ephesians 5

1 Be ye therefore followers of God, as dear children;

2 And walk in love, as Christ also hath loved us, and hath given himself for us an offering and a sacrifice to God for a sweetsmelling savour.

3 But fornication, and all uncleanness, or covetousness, let it not be once named among you, as becometh saints;

4 Neither filthiness, nor foolish talking, nor jesting, which are not convenient: but rather giving of thanks.

5 For this ye know, that no whoremonger, nor unclean person, nor covetous man, who is an idolater, hath any inheritance in the kingdom of Christ and of God.

. . . .

21 Submitting yourselves one to another in the fear of God.

22 Wives, submit yourselves unto your own husbands, as unto the Lord.

23 For the husband is the head of the wife, even as Christ is the head of the church: and he is the savior of the body.

24 Therefore as the church is subject unto Christ, so let the wives be to their own husbands in every thing.

25 Husbands, love your wives, even as Christ also loved the church, and gave himself for it;

26 That he might sanctify and cleanse it with the washing of water by the word,

27 That he might present it to himself a glorious church, not having spot, or wrinkle, or any such thing; but that it should be holy and without blemish.

28 So ought men to love their wives as their own bodies. He that loveth his wife loveth himself.

29 For no man ever yet hated his own flesh; but nourisheth and cherisheth it, even as the Lord the church.

. . . .

Ephesians 6

1 Children, obey your parents in the Lord: for this is right.

2 Honour thy father and mother; which is the first commandment with promise;

3 That it may be well with thee, and thou mayest live long on the earth.

4 And, ye fathers, provoke not your children to wrath: but bring them up in the nurture and admonition of the Lord.

■ THE LESSON EXPLAINED

Responsible to Be Pure (5:1–5)　　1473

People in Christ with His spiritual gifts have to do more than just exercise those gifts all the time. They have to live in relationship to other people. How does Christ want you to relate to people? Paul quickly ticked off the ways: follow God; be His obedient children, not self-serving grown-ups; love every person you deal with with the kind of love Christ had as He died on the cross for your sins; leave out the things the world delights in such as sexual sins that make you unclean before God and make you desire ever more "forbidden love." You are set apart to God, not set apart to fulfill your fleshly appetites.

Watch what you say. You may think it is in fun, but if it hurts another rather than building up another person, then it is wrong. Filthy talk does not belong in a saint's mouth; neither do sexual innuendos or jokes. What fits the Christian's mouth is thanksgiving, praise to God for what He has done for you. Such honors God, helps you, and lifts up other people. Do not fool yourself. Your acts and speech show who you are. If the above acts and talk dominate your life, you do not belong to God and have no hope of heaven.

Responsible in Married Love (5:21–29)

How you relate to your marriage partner says much about how you relate to Christ. You commit yourself to the other person, wanting the best for the mate because of your reverence for and relationship to God. Wives let husbands take the lead just as they let Christ direct their lives. Remember, Christ died to save you from hell. God has set up a family organization, with the husband responsible for the family, and thus the leader in the family. Not even a small family can function without a recognized leader. Following the husband's lead is a moral responsibility for the wife who recognizes her freedom to make moral choices under God.

Wives submit to a certain kind of husband/leader. This one loves the wife as much as Christ loved the church, enough to die for. Christ wanted to make the church perfect. The husband's leadership has no selfish motives at all. The husband does nothing that would approach harming the wife. The husband keeps the wife protected and perfect for Christ.

Responsible in Family Life (6:1–4)

Husbands and wives produce children. What role should children play in family life? They should respect and honor their parents. Parents acting as Paul described in the preceding verses certainly deserve such respect. Children should apply the Ten Commandments to themselves and honor parents, knowing they will receive God's blessings. This happens when fathers take family lead correctly, do nothing to provoke anger and hatred in the family, but instead lead their children to know, love, and serve God. This is responsible living.

■ TRUTHS TO LIVE BY

Believers have responsibilities. Being a Christian is more than making a public profession of faith and waiting for heaven time to come. Being a Christian is a daily opportunity to obey God in love and carry out family responsibilities in a way that shows God's self-giving love to the world.

Believers show love in every area of life. Showing love is a believer's major responsibility. When selfless, self-giving love dominates every relationship and every action, the believer will fulfill all other responsibilities to Christ and will help family and church mature in Him.

Believers live out Christ's love in family relationships. Family relationships can be a continual warfare, each member seeking personal rights and each wanting to dominate the others. In Christ, family relationships have an organization that gives leadership to the husband but also gives him the greatest responsibility—loving the family enough to die for it.

■ A VERSE TO REMEMBER

Submitting yourselves one to another in the fear of God.—Ephesians 5:21

■ DAILY BIBLE READINGS

July 17 — Turn Your Backs on Pagan Ways. Eph. 5:1–5
July 18 — Live as Children of the Light. Eph. 5:6–14
July 19 — Serve and Worship with Thanks. Eph. 5:15–20
July 20 — Words for Christians in Families. Eph. 5:21–27
July 21 — Love as Christ Loved the Church. Eph. 5:28–33
July 22 — Treat Everyone with Love and Respect. Eph. 6:1–9
July 23 — Hear God's Word, and Obey. Luke 6:43–49

1287

Called to Stand Firm

Basic Passage: Ephesians 6:10–24

God's power became real in Kenya. No more talking about something that seldom happened and certainly was not expected. In Kenya people came to you wanting to hear the gospel. You testified and expected everyone who heard to accept Christ. You prayed and knew people would be healed. You found tormented lives and expected demons to fly before God's power. God's power worked as God's people stood firm, for other powers fought furiously. Witchcraft and demonic practices join Islam and its millions of oil dollars in a last-ditch effort to stamp out Christianity and control eastern Africa. Believers have to know on whose side they stand and stand firm.

■ THE BIBLE LESSON

Ephesians 6

10 Finally, my brethren, be strong in the Lord, and in the power of his might.

1 Put on the whole armour of God, that ye may be able to stand against the wiles of the devil.

12 For we wrestle not against flesh and blood, but against principalities, against powers, against the rulers of the darkness of this world, against spiritual wickedness in high places.

13 Wherefore take unto you the whole armor of God, that ye may be able to withstand in the evil day, and having done all, to stand.

14 Stand therefore, having your loins girt about with truth, and having on the breastplate of righteousness;

15 And your feet shod with the preparation of the gospel of peace;

16 Above all, taking the shield of faith, wherewith ye shall be able to quench all the fiery darts of the wicked.

17 And take the helmet of salvation, and the sword of the Spirit, which is the word of God:

18 Praying always with all prayer and supplication in the Spirit, and watching thereunto with all perseverance and supplication for all saints;

19 And for me, that utterance may be given unto me, that I may open my mouth boldly, to make known the mystery of the gospel,

20 For which I am an ambassador in bonds: that therein I may speak boldly, as I ought to speak.

21 But that ye also may know my affairs, and how I do, Tychicus, a beloved brother and faithful minister in the Lord, shall make known to you all things:

22 Whom I have sent unto you for the same purpose, that ye might know our affairs, and that he might comfort your hearts.

23 Peace be to the brethren, and love with faith, from God the Father and the Lord Jesus Christ.

24 Grace be with all them that love our Lord Jesus Christ in sincerity. Amen.

■ THE LESSON EXPLAINED

Use God's Power (6:10–12)

Paul asked the Ephesian believers for a lot: unity, faith, loving use of spiritual gifts, responsible social and family living, a higher moral code than anyone in their society. How could all this happen? Paul closed his letter by reminding the readers of God's resources they could call on and their need to rely faithfully on those resources. You have strength, only not in yourselves. It comes from God. You are in a fight to the finish with Satan and his forces, so you need protection and weapons. God has supplied them. Put them on, or you will lose the battle. Supernatural forces and political forces oppose you. Depend on God's power.

Wear God's Armor (6:13–17)

Remember each piece of armor God makes available. You will need it to stand against such enemies. You have the truth. The enemy tells lies. You do the right, moral, good things. The enemy does only evil. You have the gospel of peace, reconciling all people. The enemy knows only the strategy of war, pitting people against each other. You have faith in God. Nothing the deceiving enemy throws at you can hit its mark. You have salvation for eternity. The enemy has only eternal torment in hell. You have God's holy Word, brought to mind by the Spirit in you. The enemy has only words of temptation, trying to throw you off course and into defeat. Choose your weapons: God's or the enemy's. Put them on.

Pray for God's Saints (6:18–24)

Armor on, weapons in hand, go to war. Look at God's strategy: prayer. The entire church of God is at war with Satan. Pray all the time for all the saints. Depend on the Spirit to lead you to what you must pray for. Pray for me that I may witness to God's Good News as He wants me to. I may be in prison; still, I represent God and His salvation to those I meet. Pray for me. I'll let you know how your prayers are being answered. I am sending the faithful Tychicus (see Acts 20:4; Col. 4:7–9; 2 Tim. 4:12; Titus 3:12) to share the news with you. If you stand firm, then God's peace and love will control your lives, and God's grace will provide all you need. Put on the armor. Pray. Stand firm. Do not let the enemy win over you.

■ TRUTHS TO LIVE BY

God supplies all the power and resources you need to face life's troubles. Life is not easy. In a Roman prison, Paul certainly knew that. Still, he knew how to face the harshest circumstances. Trust God, use His resources, and pray. You can do the same. It works.

God equips you to fight Satan. You do not have to be an apostle like Paul to gain Satan's attention. He opposes everyone who claims Jesus as Savior. He is attacking you if you are representing Christ. Only God's equipment can ensure you will win the battle.

God uses your prayers as resources for others. As part of God's team, you supply resources for others in their fight against Satan and for God. God uses your prayers to bring power and hope and deliverance to others. Pray!

■ A VERSE TO REMEMBER

Finally, my brethren, be strong in the Lord, and in the power of his might.—Ephesians 6:10

■ DAILY BIBLE READINGS

July 24 — Be Strong in the Lord. Eph. 6:10–15
July 25 — Pray Always in the Lord's Spirit. Eph. 6:16–20
July 26 — Grace, Peace, and Love from God. Eph. 6:21–24
July 27 — God's Spirit Will Strengthen You. John 14:15–27
July 28 — Abide in Christ, and Bear Fruit. John 15:1–11
July 29 — We Are Chosen by Christ. John 15:12–27
July 30 — Your Pain Will Turn to Rejoicing. John 16:16–24

The Supremacy of Christ

Basic Passage: Colossians 1:15–28

Sat down on a short stone fence around one of the nicest houses I saw in the region of Busia, Kenya. The Kenyan pastor summoned the two young men to come and listen to the American visitor. Unsuspecting, I quietly, confidently gave my testimony to how Jesus loved me, died for me, and promised me resurrection. Then the second young man ran into the house and returned with a book, the Koran. He wanted to show me the real truth, the truth that came after Jesus did. A forty-five minute conversation ensued. I found myself digging deep to find and explain who Jesus is for me. Today's world gives you many opportunities to tell others that Jesus is supreme over every other power and religion in the world.

■ THE BIBLE LESSON

Colossians 1

15 Who is the image of the invisible God, the firstborn of every creature:

16 For by him were all things created, that are in heaven, and that are in earth, visible and invisible, whether they be thrones, or dominions, or principalities, or powers: all things were created by him, and for him:

17 And he is before all things, and by him all things consist.

18 And he is the head of the body, the church: who is the beginning, the firstborn from the dead; that in all things he might have the preeminence.

19 For it pleased the Father that in him should all fullness dwell;

20 And, having made peace through the blood of his cross, by him to reconcile all things unto himself; by him, I say, whether they be things in earth, or things in heaven.

21 And you, that were sometime alienated and enemies in your mind by wicked works, yet now hath he reconciled

22 In the body of his flesh through death, to present you holy and unblameable and unreproveable in his sight:

23 If ye continue in the faith grounded and settled, and be not moved away from the hope of the gospel, which ye have heard, and which was preached to every creature which is under heaven; whereof I Paul am made a minister;

24 Who now rejoice in my sufferings for you, and fill up that which is behind of the afflictions of Christ in my flesh for his body's sake, which is the church:

25 Whereof I am made a minister, according to the dispensation of God which is given to me for you, to fulfil the word of God;

26 Even the mystery which hath been hid from ages and from generations, but now is made manifest to his saints:

27 To whom God would make known what is the riches of the glory of this mystery among the Gentiles; which is Christ in you, the hope of glory:

28 Whom we preach, warning every man, and teaching every man in all wisdom; that we may present every man perfect in Christ Jesus.

■ THE LESSON EXPLAINED

The Image of the Creator (1:15–17)

Who are you? Members of Christ's kingdom (1:13), redeemed by His blood and forgiven of your sins (1:14). That means you ought to know as much about Christ as possible. Everything in your life depends on Him. Paul gave you a hymn about Christ to let you know who He is.

He is the image of the invisible God. God created us in His image (Gen. 1:26, 27). We ruined that image and did not represent God to the world as we should. Thus, God sent His Son Jesus, who was the perfect, exact image of God and maintained that image without sin. This Son is eternal, existing before creation itself. He is unique, unlike any part of creation, for He is God become flesh. He was God's intermediary, God's instrument in fashioning the world. He established the world's institutions, and so has power over all of them. Nothing would exist if Christ had not joined the Father in creating it.

The Head of the Church (1:18,19)

Christ as image of God makes Himself known on earth through His body, the church. As He incarnated God on earth, the church incarnates Him. God raised Christ from the dead, giving Christ the place of highest respect, authority, and power in the universe. Why is this true? Because everything that makes God, God, lives in Christ. He has all the fulness, all the components of God. He is the Creator God come in human flesh to die and be raised. You need fear no earthly power. Christ is over all.

The Source of Reconciliation (1:20–24)

You had no reason to expect anything from this God become flesh, this preeminent one over all the earth. In love He chose to bring you back to God, to restore the connection sin broke. He died on the cross to do this. Now you can stand in God's presence with no one condemning you. He looks at you through Christ's blood and sees you as pure, clean, and holy.

What is your part in all this? Keep the faith. Do not turn to powers of the world in fear and frustration. Trust Christ. He will save you as He promised. His gospel is aimed at the whole world. You know how I have tried to preach it everywhere because God called me to. I am His servant. I suffer for Him gladly; in fact, I rejoice that He would give me opportunity to suffer. Such sufferings are part of what Christ has called the church to do and be, to take up our cross for Him. Such sufferings point to the last days, when the time of suffering will be over and Christ will reward His church eternally. Until then I and the church must suffer as He suffered. As we, the body of Christ, suffers, He also suffers and will do so until the second coming. Let us suffer, so He may come.

The Mystery of God (1:25–28)

God purposed in eternity before creation to save people through the suffering of His Son. He sent Jesus to the cross to fulfill that plan. Until Jesus came, that plan was a mystery the world neither knew nor understood. The early church learned the meaning of the mystery of God's eternal plan of salvation from Jesus. On the Damascus road, Paul learned the mystery and became its minister, telling all people that God's eternal salvation was now available through Christ. The mysterious eternal plan was not limited to Jews. It included Gentiles, too. All have hope for eternal life with Christ in heaven because Jesus died for all. So we preach the gospel, calling all people to accept Christ as Savior and warning all people to live in obedience to Christ until He comes again. Then we want every person to stand before Christ's judgment throne as mature Christians. We have not yet reached maturity. Even Paul kept striving to do so, but we must not give up the fight. Put Christ above all. Let Him create His image in you.

■ TRUTHS TO LIVE BY

Christ is God's eternal image. Christ shows us perfectly what God is like. Thus, Christ is God and has all the power and authority of God. Look to Christ to know God.

Christ's death is the source of your life. God developed a mysterious plan we would never have created: give salvation to people by letting the Son of God die on the cross. You can truly live now and in eternity only when Christ lives in you.

Christ is the head of the church. Christ died to create the church. He wants you to be part of that church and bring that church to perfect maturity, each part of the body doing its part. What is your part?

Christ is the basis for your eternal hope. Do you know for sure you are going to heaven when you die? You can! Trust Christ. He will save you for eternity and give you assurance that you belong to Him forever.

■ A VERSE TO REMEMBER

For it pleased the Father that in him should all fulness dwell; And, having made peace through the blood of his cross, by him to reconcile all things unto himself; by him, I say, whether they be things in earth, or things in heaven.—Colossians 1:19, 20

■ DAILY BIBLE READINGS

July 31 — Paul Gives Thanks for the Colossians. Col. 1:1–8

Aug. 1 — Paul Prays for the Colossian Christians. Col. 1:9–14

Aug. 2 — The Fullness of God Dwelled in Christ. Col. 1:15–20

Aug. 3 — God's Mystery Revealed to the Saints. Col. 1:21–29

Aug. 4 — Jesus Christ: God's Word and Light. John 1:1–9

Aug. 5 — God's Word Lived Among Us. John 1:10–18

Aug. 6 — Christ Is Superior Even to Angels. Heb. 1:1–14

A Complete Life in Christ

Basic Passage: Colossians 2:6–19

Emptying the nest and losing my wife created an identity crisis for me. I am no longer constantly encountering friends of my boys who identify me as their father. Fathering has become only a sometime job, so I do not see myself very often as mainly a father. No longer a husband, I do not identify myself in relationship to Mary. Has my life been so emptied and robbed of relationships that I no longer have identity? No! I still have the central relationship in life. I belong to Christ. I can know the complete life in Him.

■ THE BIBLE LESSON

Colossians 2

6 As ye have therefore received Christ Jesus the Lord, so walk ye in him:

7 Rooted and built up in him, and established in the faith, as ye have been taught, abounding therein with thanksgiving.

8 Beware lest any man spoil you through philosophy and vain deceit, after the tradition of men, after the rudiments of the world, and not after Christ.

9 For in him dwelleth all the fulness of the Godhead bodily.

10 And ye are complete in him, which is the head of all principality and power:

11 In whom also ye are circumcised with the circumcision made without hands, in putting off the body of the sins of the flesh by the circumcision of Christ:

12 Buried with him in baptism, wherein also ye are risen with him through the faith of the operation of God, who hath raised him from the dead.

13 And you, being dead in your sins and the uncircumcision of your flesh, hath he quickened together with him, having forgiven you all trespasses;

14 *Blotting out the handwriting of ordinances that was against us, which was contrary to us, and took it out of the way, nailing it to his cross;*

15 *And having spoiled principalities and powers, he made a shew of them openly, triumphing over them in it.*

16 *Let no man therefore judge you in meat, or in drink, or in respect of an holyday, or of the new moon, or of the sabbath days:*

17 *Which are a shadow of things to come; but the body is of Christ.*

18 *Let no man beguile you of your reward in a voluntary humility and worshipping of angels, intruding into those things which he hath not seen, vainly puffed up by his fleshly mind,*

19 *And not holding the Head, from which all the body by joints and bands having nourishment ministered, and knit together, increaseth with the increase of God.*

■ THE LESSON EXPLAINED

Christ: The Way You Walk (2:6–8)

Temptations surround you. People have new answers to your life problems every day. Turn a deaf ear. You already know the answers. Christ answers every need you have. Walk in His way. Don't just talk about Jesus. Obey Him, and walk daily with Him. Listen to what you have learned about Christ. Let it make you mature in Him. Let it give you stability so you do not run after every new teaching. Be thankful for Christ and what He gives you each day. Your choice: human teachings or Christ's? Which will you follow?

Christ: The Source of Your Completeness (2:9–14)

Listen to the case for Christ. Every element of God lives in Christ. He is God in person for you. He is the head of the body, so He supplies everything you, as a part of the body, need. Don't look back to Judaism and its rites and rituals. Christ perfected Judaism. He took care of sins in a way

Judaism never could. You were baptized into Christ's death and resurrection. Let that control your life. He has cleansed you, forgiven you of your sins. Yes, He nailed every sin you've ever committed to Christ's cross. You are complete in Jesus. How can you ask for more?

Christ: The Head of Your Unity (2:15–19)

The cross of Christ changed world history. It showed that no political or military leaders have control. Christ defeated all of them and their selfish ambitions on the cross. He took away power from all religious leaders who would make you follow certain rules and laws to get to heaven. What you eat or drink or how you behave on the Sabbath or other festival days is not the important thing. Don't feel condemned because someone else does not approve of the way you disobey their rules. These all foreshadowed Jesus' coming. Now He is here. Forget the shadows. Follow Jesus.

Do not let someone convince you they have some secret religious knowledge, some access to angels that you must learn and practice. Such people are proud but wrong, following the flesh, not the Spirit. All you need is Jesus. Want to grow spiritually? Forget rituals and secret knowledge. Jesus is the head of the body. He feeds each of its members. He lets you grow in the way God wants you to grow. What else can you ask? Follow Jesus, and add nothing to Him.

■ TRUTHS TO LIVE BY

Christ is superior to all human philosophies. Human philosophers recognize life's mysteries and offer tentative solutions to them. Christ is the agent of creation who knows all life's mysteries. Want answers? Follow Jesus.

Christ supplies everything you need for a complete life. Religions come up with all sorts of gimmicks to impress and entice you. They try to make you feel superior to other people. Only One is superior. That is Christ. Follow Him. He has everything you need and wants to give it to you.

Christ is your only judge. Everywhere you go, people want to judge you, to show you that they have a better way, they know better rules, they have secret information. The Bible says, Jesus is the Way. Do not worry about any one else condemning or judging you for any reason. Be concerned only that you will stand mature in Christ at the final judgment where He is judge over all.

■ A VERSE TO REMEMBER

As ye have therefore received Christ Jesus the Lord, so walk ye in him: Rooted and built up in him, and established in the faith, as ye have been taught, abounding therein with thanksgiving.—Colossians 2:6, 7

■ DAILY BIBLE READINGS

Aug. 7 — Paul Commends the Colossian Christians.
           Col. 2:1–5
Aug. 8 — God Dwells Fully in Jesus Christ. Col. 2:6–10
Aug. 9 — Dead to the Flesh, Alive in Christ. Col. 2:11–16
Aug. 10 — Hold Fast to Christ, Our Head. Col. 2:17–23
Aug. 11 — Jesus: Mediator of a New Covenant. Heb. 8:1–7
Aug. 12 — The Blood of Christ Purifies Us. Heb. 9:11–15
Aug. 13 — Christ Perfected Those Who Are Sanctified.
           Heb. 10:11–18

The Way to Righteousness

Basic Passage: Colossians 3:1–3, 5–17

"Pray for me. My husband spends all his time with his two wives in Uganda. He never comes back to spend time with me here in Kenya. Pray that God will make him come back to me." Such words from a sad young woman reminded me of the privilege to live in a country where God's righteous ways are at least known. Kenya reveals a new way of life, totally separated from God. Sexual morals are unknown. One of four people are said to be HIV positive. Women have no hope of escaping the domineering rule of men, who sit in the village talking while women raise crops and family. Kenya reminds me anew of how much all of us need to know the way of righteousness.

■ THE BIBLE LESSON

Colossians 3

1 If ye then be risen with Christ, seek those things which are above, where Christ sitteth on the right hand of God.

2 Set your affection on things above, not on things on the earth.

3 For ye are dead, and your life is hid with Christ in God.

5 Mortify therefore your members which are upon the earth; fornication, uncleanness, inordinate affection, evil concupiscence, and covetousness, which is idolatry:

6 For which things' sake the wrath of God cometh on the children of disobedience:

7 In the which ye also walked sometime, when ye lived in them.

8 But now ye also put off all these; anger, wrath, malice, blasphemy, filthy communication out of your mouth.

9 Lie not one to another, seeing that ye have put off the old man with his deeds;

10 And have put on the new man, which is renewed in knowledge after the image of him that created him:

11 Where there is neither Greek nor Jew, circumcision nor uncircumcision, Barbarian, Scythian, bond nor free: but Christ is all, and in all.

12 Put on therefore, as the elect of God, holy and beloved, bowels of mercies, kindness, humbleness of mind, meekness, long-suffering;

13 Forbearing one another, and forgiving one another, if any man have a quarrel against any: even as Christ forgave you, so also do ye.

14 And above all these things put on charity, which is the bond of perfectness.

15 And let the peace of God rule in your hearts, to the which also ye are called in one body; and be ye thankful.

16 Let the word of Christ dwell in you richly in all wisdom; teaching and admonishing one another in psalms and hymns and spiritual songs, singing with grace in your hearts to the Lord.

17 And whatsoever ye do in word or deed, do all in the name of the Lord Jesus, giving thanks to God and the Father by him.

THE LESSON EXPLAINED

Christ: Your Heavenly Target (3:1–3)

Do you trust Christ for salvation? Does that mean that, as your baptism symbolized, you have been buried with Him to sin and raised to a new life? Then life has a new goal, a new target. You look up to Christ, not out to the world, to find your way of life. You desire to fulfill heaven's expectations, not earth's. You have died to the old life. Your life is not buried in worldly activities. You are hidden from the world's ways. You are in Christ.

Christ: Your Reason to Forsake Sin (3:5–10)

Dead to sin in Christ! Live it out. Get rid of sexual sin. Quit giving in to the lusts of your body. Bury them with Christ. To serve the desires of your body is to make your body your god. That is the sin of idolatry. Bury it. Such sins bring God's wrath. Look what happened to the kings of Israel and Judah so long ago. They felt His wrath. Must you, too? That is the old, before-Christ way. Christ gives you reason and power to give up the sins of your old life. Treat others right. Do not make them objects of your anger, hatred, foul language and cursing, and lies. One buried with Christ does not act like that. You act like a new man; you show the world God's image.

Christ: The Purpose for Your Living (3:11–17)

Your background makes no difference. Who your parents were or what your race is doesn't matter. Christ is everything. He buries all human differences to make us all alike, free from sin, in Him. Dress up in His clothing so you will look like Him. He is kind to everyone, concerned for their needs, putting them before His reputation, bending to help them rather than standing to draw attention to Himself, patient and willing to wait, putting up with the weaknesses and obnoxious qualities the other has and forgiving them for hurting, even crucifying Him. Live like that. Forgive. Don't fight. Don't argue. Live in love. This shows you are becoming mature in Him. Loving the other does not let you get angry or do the other things the world does. Let God's peace maintain unity in the church, so you do not argue or get angry with Christian brothers. God's Word can control your life, so you can act like Christ. Worship together and learn from each other how better to serve Christ. Let every action be something you do to bring honor to Christ and to represent Him to the world. If you honor Christ in what you do, then you are walking the way of righteousness.

■ TRUTHS TO LIVE BY

Salvation in Christ means you have given up old habits.
You have no excuse. You do not have to be like that. Christ
cleanses and forgives. He changes lives. Trust Him to
change yours. Then leave old habits behind.

*Salvation in Christ means you seek to live in His love per-
fectly.* Giving up old habits means acquiring new ones.
Christ should be the only source of your habits. Let His love
fill you. Live in love for others as He did. Let no other standard satisfy you.

*Salvation in Christ means you obey His Word and no
other.* How can you know if you are living in His love? Read
His Word. It shows you constantly the qualities of life Christ
lived and wants you to live. Measure yourself by the Word
and by nothing else.

■ A VERSE TO REMEMBER

*And whatsoever ye do in word or deed, do all in the name
of the Lord Jesus, giving thanks to God and the Father by
him.—Colossians 3:17*

■ DAILY BIBLE READINGS

Aug. 14 — Revealed with Christ in Glory. Col. 3:1–6
Aug. 15 — Put on the New Self. Col. 3:7–11
Aug. 16 — Live Faithfully, Joyfully, and Give Thanks.
Col. 3:12–17
Aug. 17 — Love and Honor All People. Col. 3:18–4:1
Aug. 18 — Live and Speak in Christian Love. Col. 4:2–6
Aug. 19 — Paul's Faithful Support Community.
Col. 4:7–11
Aug. 20 — Paul's Final Greetings to the Colossians.
Col. 4:12–18

Welcoming Others in Christ

Basic Passage: Philemon 4–21

Angry, alone, hurt, confused, abandoned. The young man trembled against my shoulder as he told of his feelings—feelings brought on by a father who never abused him, simply ignored him. The father was so busy doing God's work in a foreign land that he never took time to listen to his son. Finally, the son had dutifully traveled more than a thousand miles to come to school where Dad wanted him to go. Now son wanted to know how to find reconciliation with a father so far away geographically and emotionally. How can we cut through such emotional scars to experience reconciliation? Onesimus had a similar desire for reconciliation but in far different circumstances.

THE BIBLE LESSON

Philemon

4 I thank my God, making mention of thee always in my prayers,

5 Hearing of thy love and faith, which thou hast toward the Lord Jesus, and toward all saints;

6 That the communication of thy faith may become effectual by the acknowledging of every good thing which is in you in Christ Jesus.

7 For we have great joy and consolation in thy love, because the bowels of the saints are refreshed by thee, brother.

8 Wherefore, though I might be much bold in Christ to enjoin thee that which is convenient,

9 Yet for love's sake I rather beseech thee, being such an one as Paul the aged, and now also a prisoner of Jesus Christ.

10 I beseech thee for my son Onesimus, whom I have begotten in my bonds:

11 Which in time past was to thee unprofitable, but now profitable to thee and to me:

12 Whom I have sent again: thou therefore receive him, that is, mine own bowels:

13 Whom I would have retained with me, that in thy stead he might have ministered unto me in the bonds of the gospel:

14 But without thy mind would I do nothing; that thy benefit should not be as it were of necessity, but willingly.

15 For perhaps he therefore departed for a season, that thou shouldest receive him for ever;

16 Not now as a servant, but above a servant, a brother beloved, specially to me, but how much more unto thee, both in the flesh, and in the Lord?

17 If thou count me therefore a partner, receive him as myself.

18 If he hath wronged thee, or oweth thee ought, put that on mine account;

19 I Paul have written it with mine own hand, I will repay it: albeit I do not say to thee how thou owest unto me even thine own self besides.

20 Yea, brother, let me have joy of thee in the Lord: refresh my bowels in the Lord.

21 Having confidence in thy obedience I wrote unto thee, knowing that thou wilt also do more than I say.

■ THE LESSON EXPLAINED

The Joy You Bring (4–7)

A new friend brought joy to Paul's life, but sorrow, too. Somehow in a Roman prison, Paul met Onesimus, a slave on the run. In God's providence, Paul knew the person who caused Onesimus's concern. That was Philemon, a member of the church, apparently in Colossae. So Paul wrote a letter, seeking to bring a new Christian slave back into good graces with his Christian master. Prayer was the beginning point. Paul prayed continually for Philemon, giving thanks for who Philemon was, a person who loved Christ and showed love to the church. Paul prayed that Philemon's faith leading to such expressions of love might help him understand and experience the blessings and generosity of Christ. Then he would be ready to respond to Paul's request and would bring Christ's joy to himself, to Paul, and to the church.

The Joy You Can Bring (8–16)

Knowing the joy and power another person can bring to the church gives us boldness to make requests of the person. Paul summoned up all His Christian courage to ask Philemon to do the unthinkable: restore his slave without the normal cruel punishment. Let Onesimus be to you what his name means: profitable. Let Onesimus, the new convert to Christ, represent my joy and my deepest desires. If you love me, accept him. He could be very profitable to me here as a minister of God's gospel, but I send him back where he belongs to bring back the reconciliation that you both need to experience with one another in Christ.

That reconciliation will tie you together in a whole new relationship, far above that of master and slave. No, no matter the economic social relationships you have, you will be brothers in Christ. Oh, the joy you will bring me and the Lord if you will receive your disobedient slave as a brother in Christ!

The Joy You Bring to Christ (17–21)

I am counting on your relationship with me. We have always been partners in God's gospel. Show your partnership by doing what I am asking. If he owes you something, take it off his account and charge it to mine. I am right now signing the bill. Of course, I will not take into account that you owe your very life in Christ to my testimony to you. Oh, bring joy to me and particularly to Christ our Lord by doing this most difficult favor for me and for Him. I know your Christian witness and faith, so I know you will do what I ask. Then joy will flood all our souls. Welcome Onesimus in Christ. You will be welcoming me and the Lord.

■ TRUTHS TO LIVE BY

Love creates joy in others. When we express Christian love through acts of kindness and gifts of love, we bring joy to many other people. Christian faith seeks to enrich others with Christ's joy.

Love asks difficult favors of others in Christ. Christian love is bold. It does not seek to know what others will think. It seeks only the mind of Christ. Thus, Christian love does what Christ would do—invite others to act boldly in Christ's name to do what is right in His sight.

Love expects Christlike responses from others. Love in Christ depends on unity in the body. Knowing the mind of Christ and acting boldly in obedience to that mind, Christian love trusts a fellow believer to know the mind of Christ and to respond in the way Christ would respond.

■ A VERSE TO REMEMBER

That the communication of thy faith may become effectual by the acknowledging of every good thing which is in you in Christ Jesus.—Philemon 6

■ DAILY BIBLE READINGS

Aug. 21 — Paul Gives Thanks for Philemon. Philem. 1–7
Aug. 22 — Paul Expresses His Love for Onesimus.
            Philem. 8–12
Aug. 23 — Paul Intercedes for Onesimus. Philem. 13–18
Aug. 24 — Paul's Challenge to Philemon. Philem. 19–25
Aug. 25 — Don't Let Fine Clothes Deceive You!
            James 2:1–7
Aug. 26 — Show Mercy, and Love All People. James 2:8–13
Aug. 27 — Have True Faith; Do Good Works.
            James 2:14–26

Focus on Compassion*

Basic Passage: Matthew 9:18–31, 35–36

Tears refresh the garden of ministry. I have seen it throughout life. From the squalor of government projects in west Texas where mother took me as she ministered for her Sunday school class, to the isolation of the Hispanic community where I ministered on Saturday nights in college, to the tenant farmers of Tennessee wishing they had indoor plumbing, to the coldness of enormously rich European families thriving on the goods of the world but starving for love and meaning, to the street people of Nashville sleeping on park benches, to the hungry orphans and impoverished women without money to buy medications needed to live . . . each experience has brought tears to my eyes, compassion to my heart, and prayer to my soul to find God's ways to show that all life has sanctity and worth in God's sight.

■ THE BIBLE LESSON

Matthew 9

18 While he spake these things unto them, behold, there came a certain ruler, and worshipped him, saying, My daughter is even now dead: but come and lay thy hand upon her, and she shall live.

19 And Jesus arose, and followed him, and so did his disciples.

20 And, behold, a woman, which was diseased with an issue of blood twelve years, came behind him, and touched the hem of his garment:

21 For she said within herself, If I may but touch his garment, I shall be whole.

22 But Jesus turned him about, and when he saw her, he said, Daughter, be of good comfort; thy faith hath made thee whole. And the woman was made whole from that hour.

23 And when Jesus came into the ruler's house, and saw the minstrels and the people making a noise,

24 He said unto them, Give place: for the maid is not dead, but sleepeth. And they laughed him to scorn.

25 But when the people were put forth, he went in, and took her by the hand, and the maid arose.

26 And the fame hereof went abroad into all that land.

27 And when Jesus departed thence, two blind men followed him, crying, and saying, Thou son of David, have mercy on us.

28 And when he was come into the house, the blind men came to him: and Jesus saith unto them, Believe ye that I am able to do this? They said unto him, Yea, Lord.

29 Then touched he their eyes, saying, According to your faith be it unto you.

30 And their eyes were opened; and Jesus straitly charged them, saying, See that no man know it.

31 But they, when they were departed, spread abroad his fame in all that country.

35 And Jesus went about all the cities and villages, teaching in their synagogues, and preaching the gospel of the kingdom, and healing every sickness and every disease among the people.

36 But when he saw the multitudes, he was moved with compassion on them, because they fainted, and were scattered abroad, as sheep having no shepherd.

■ THE LESSON EXPLAINED

The Worth of the Rich (9:18, 19)

Wealth and power often bring resentment. We think the person is no good because he is too far up the social or political ladder. We need to see such people in their moments of need. Christ found a leader in synagogue worship with a dying daughter. Christ ignored every characteristic of the person but one: the hurt of the moment. With compassion and care, Christ went to help a person whom God created because the person had need.

The Worth of the Hopeless (9:20–22)

On a mission of mercy, Christ found Himself interrupted. Someone else needed help and reached out to Him in desperate faith. Sick twelve years, unable to find help anywhere and at the end of her rope physically and emotionally, the woman did the unthinkable. She touched a rabbi's robes, making Him "unclean." How would Jesus react to such an audacious action? Surely, it would irritate Him to be sidetracked on His mission of mercy. No. He saw someone else in need, someone on the opposite end of the social scale. He cared for her, too, and expressed amazement at her faith. Just to touch without being seen or spoken to would make her whole, she believed. It did.

The Worth of a Child (9:23–26)

Just a little girl. What could she contribute of worth to the world in comparison to the ministry of the Son of God? Was she worth all this time, His interrupting His ministry to walk all the way to her house? He thought so. She was a human being in need. He had come to seek and to save that which was lost. He came to her. So the crowds laughed at Him. He did not come for their applause. He came to help people, for people have worth because they are people. He raised her to life. Scorn turned to wonder. The crowds spread the news.

The Worth of the Blind (9:27–31)

What a nuisance. Everywhere He went, people shouted for help. Now two more blind men, wandering helplessly across the country, hoping against hope to find some way to find new hope, new identity, new worth in life. People told them about this Jesus, one who could trace his lineage to David and could do works no one had ever done. Could this be the Messiah? Son of David, help us! Really believe I can? Oh, yes, sir! We believe. A finger reached out in care to blind eyes. If you have faith, you will see. Blind eyes opened. Don't get everyone chasing after me, now. Keep this to yourselves. Faint chance. People tell about love received and life renewed.

The Worth of the Multitudes (9:35, 36)

Just a normal day for Jesus, preaching, teaching, going to worship, finding sick people and healing them. What drove Jesus to such strenuous daily ministry? Everywhere He went, the same sight greeted Him. Hurting, hopeless, harried people lined the streets and crowded the hillsides. No direction in life, no meaning, no sense of worth, no future. Tears came to His eyes. Pain tugged at His heart. They needed someone to care, someone to see they had worth, too. Where was a shepherd for these poor, tired, lonely sheep without direction for life? Could someone find the compassion and care to bring worth to them?

■ TRUTHS TO LIVE BY

Life has worth by definition. Life is God's gift. What God gives is good. Every life, thus, is good. Every life has worth in God's sight. They should have worth in our sight. What are we doing to bring worth to the lives which so many count worthless?

People acknowledge their own worth only as we lead them to the compassionate Jesus. People with worth too often do not recognize their own worth. They see no evidence that they mean anything to anyone. When we show them Jesus' love, they find they have worth in our eyes and in His. Then they can have worth in their own eyes.

People need healing to be able to show worth to others. Once healed, the blind and the sick can share the good news of Jesus with others. They find worth in their witness and in bringing a new sense of worth to others. They find healing only as God's people bring them to Jesus and to healing power.

■ A VERSE TO REMEMBER

But when he saw the multitudes, he was moved with compassion on them, because they fainted, and were scattered abroad, as sheep having no shepherd.—Matthew 9:36

*Alternate lesson for January 16.